Life In Limbo

Life In Limbo

✦

Waiting for a Heart Transplant

Lisa Stiles Nance

iUniverse, Inc.
New York Lincoln Shanghai

Life In Limbo
Waiting for a Heart Transplant

iUniverse, Inc.

For information address:
iUniverse, Inc.
2021 Pine Lake Road, Suite 100
Lincoln, NE 68512
www.iuniverse.com

ISBN: 0-595-29772-2

Printed in the United States of America

This book is dedicated
to our donor's family—
Your brave decision
resulted in the gift of a lifetime.

Contents

Acknowledgments

I wish to thank Susan Snowden, of Snowden Editorial Services, and my friends, Mary Stearns and Eliza Bishop, for their help with editing and proofreading this book. They were also a huge support to me, always ready with encouraging words.

Also, I would like to thank Dr. Izola Young, my freshman English professor at Fayetteville State University, who recognized the writer in me when I didn't. Dr. Young, although you are gone, you will never be forgotten.

Thank you Miller, for twenty-three years of love and support. Your second chance gave me a second chance as well.

LSN
2003

Introduction

Writing about your own life is difficult. It's so tempting to sugarcoat everything so you appear to your friends and family, and anyone else who might possibly read what you've written, that you are this incredibly strong person. You don't want them to know the truth.

Truths such as when my husband, Miller, was diagnosed with congestive heart failure in 1997, with the possibility of a heart transplant looming over our heads, I wasn't strong. I was scared. When he ended up in a hospital 500 miles from home, waiting for a heart, and I found myself with everything dumped in my lap, I wasn't strong. Maybe everyone thought I was because I didn't cry on anyone's shoulder much, because I carried on, but I'm here to tell you I was wearing a big mask. I was a fake, a fraud. Every day a little part of myself crumpled. I lost my confidence. I lost my sense of humor. I broke down…a lot. But despite my gnashing of teeth and despite my bouts of martyrdom I managed to come through this experience changed in a positive way. Sometimes God has to reshape us a little and it's not a pretty sight.

After the dust settled, I knew I had to help those who would come after me, the husbands and wives of those being evaluated for heart transplants, who are at the beginning of the transplant journey. I wanted to hold up a light and say, "It's scary, but follow me; there are others like us ahead." We are the behind-the-scenes workers, keeping life going while we wait for the ultimate outcome: will he or won't he live to get a heart? We hold up the world like Atlas but feel more like Sisyphus, pushing that rock up the hill, only to have it roll back down to be pushed up again. We argue with insurance companies and deal with angry teenagers. We post-date checks and sell our jewelry. We go on anti-depressants and gain weight. We wear a plastic smile and tell everyone else how it's going to be all right. We do these things and make decisions alone. In the meantime, we silently fall apart.

Along the way I learned many lessons. And I couldn't help coming away from the experience with a new admiration for single parents, widows and widowers, spouses of deployed military personnel, and anyone taking care of a sick relative full-time. They deal with the loss of a partner every single day. For them, there is no light at the end of the tunnel. They just learn to accept things and deal with them.

I was insulated for the 18-plus years of my marriage. I had a partner to lean on and share the trials and tribulations of raising two children and paying bills and keeping a house and all the other stuff life is made of. I was living in a cushy environment that didn't expect me to make too many big decisions alone. There was always someone else to bounce ideas off. And there are thousands, probably millions, of women just like me. But suddenly, in one remarkable instant, my comfortable existence was obliterated. Fear and doubt slid under the door. Anger and sorrow seeped into the woodwork. But I learned to deal with it. And now I want to help others in the same or other crisis situations learn how to deal with their experiences too.

The Last Kiss

One day we'll kiss
for the last time
and we won't even know it.
We won't know
our time together
is over.
We'll think it's just like
any other day—
just another kiss,
in a lifetime of kisses.
We won't savor it,
pressing firmly
or fervently
or try to hold on
as long as we can.
Because we won't know
it's the last
kiss.

1

o o o o o o o o o o o o o o o o o o o o o o o o o o o o o o o o o o o

"You can't have a testimony without a test."

—*Iyanla Vanzant*

THE JOURNEY BEGINS

There were only three days left until the new millennium. The last Christmas of the last century had come and gone and my husband, Miller, and I were slow dancing in the darkened rec room. Outside, snow tapped on the windows, glistening under the illumination of hundreds of city lights. We were eleven floors above the street, inside one of the country's most prestigious medical centers. He was attached to a mobile I.V. pole by a narrow plastic tube that entered his chest and transported a life-sustaining drug called dobutamine to the interior of his heart. I clung to his scrawny body, my arms wrapped around his neck, my body pressed as close as I could get, and as we swayed to the music we entered a suspended moment, where we were allowed to forget that time was running out.

Miller had been in the hospital since July and on the transplant list since August. The question that had begun as "When will he get a heart?" had now turned into "Will he live long enough to get a heart?" Our journey towards transplant was about to exceed the average amount of time most recipients wait and our hope was holding on by a golden strand. We had rejoiced with the lucky ones when they received their new organs and we had shared the sorrow of the loved ones of those who couldn't out wait the wait. By now the wondering, the hoping, the praying had become a way of life as familiar as breathing, yet the waiting was still like a new wound, painful and omnipresent. Little did we know, as we held each other for dear life in the stillness of that rec room that our wait was about to end.

DIAGNOSIS

Our journey to transplant began long before Miller's name went on the transplant list. It was his diagnosis of congestive heart failure that was the first domino to fall. It came in April 1997. We had moved to Lenoir, a small town in the foothills of the Blue Ridge Mountains, the year before from Fayetteville, North Carolina. We were living our dream. Living in the mountains, owning our own businesses, raising our children in this beautiful place. We rented a house fifteen miles from town. It was quiet, secluded and surrounded on all sides by thick woods, with a view of the foothills in the distance. To this day, I will always believe God put us in this place because He knew what was ahead.

The house was charming, the surroundings tranquil. In the morning, deer grazed in the pasture in front of the house and at night, the sky was a blanket of stars. Our landlady, a retired English teacher and dean of the local community college, was like an old friend I had known for years. We could talk for hours about all my favorite subjects: books, writing, and nature. In the months to come, this place would become my haven and my sanctuary.

One year after moving to Lenoir, almost to the day, Miller got sick. We thought he had a virus or the flu because he had the usual aching and fever that accompanies those kinds of sicknesses. He also had a terrible cough that, even after the fever went away, would not disappear. On the contrary, it got worse, keeping Miller from sleeping and causing soreness in his ribs and stomach. I had listened to his smoker's hack for our entire married life, but noticed that the cough he now had was different, deeper.

As the coughing grew worse, Miller began to get weaker and weaker. The usual tasks, such as climbing the basement stairs, working on his car, or taking out the trash, became increasingly difficult. He was tired all the time and began taking naps, something he had never done before.

The symptoms were so subtle and so much like a common virus, he just continued to try to carry on. When I would mention that maybe he should go to the doctor he just brushed the suggestion off. But as his breathing became more and more labored, he finally realized he was sicker than he thought and he consented to getting it checked out.

For over two hours, I sat in the waiting room of the doctor's office wondering what was wrong. Why was it taking so long? I've always had a strong imagination and so I conjured up one disease after another that Miller could possibly have, including the "Big C." After another half an hour I couldn't wait any longer. I went to the receptionist's desk and opened the door to the exam area. There stood Miller talking to the bookkeeper. He looked at me. I knew something was wrong. He said, "I'm a very sick boy, Lisa."

My insides felt hollow. "What is it?" I asked.

"It's my heart," he replied.

That same day we met with a cardiologist. He outlined the tests Miller would have in the next few days, ending with an electrocardiogram on Friday. On Monday, we would meet with him again for the results. Needless to say, that weekend was the longest one we'd ever lived through.

On Monday, the cardiologist looked at Miller and said, "You have an enlarged heart. It's causing you to have congestive heart failure." He went on to explain that congestive heart failure (CHF) develops when the pumping chambers of the heart contract poorly and do not supply adequate circulation to the vital organs. The poor pumping action causes blood and fluid buildup, or congestion, in the organs. The main organs being affected at that moment for Miller were his lungs.

At the age of thirty-eight, Miller was extremely young to develop CHF and our first question was how could this have happened to him. I was especially surprised because in our eighteen years of marriage, Miller had never taken a day of sick leave from work. He just never got sick. The cardiologist explained to us there are three things that can cause heart enlargement: a blockage in the coronary arteries, a viral infection, or poisoning by toxins, including alcohol. After reviewing the tests, he had ruled out any blockages; that left a viral infection or poisoning. I believe it was probably a little of both. The doctor didn't rule out either one.

Miller loved his beer. And like millions of others he drank after work and on weekends. Now, he would have to quit drinking any alcoholic beverages forever, if he wanted his heart to get better with the assistance of medication. And the smoking would have to stop as well.

"We caught this just in time," the doctor said. "Right now, you're sitting on the fence; you could go either way. The best-case scenario is that your heart could get better in four or five years, if you take the medicine, exercise, and don't drink or smoke. The worst-case scenario is that the heart could get worse and you would need a heart transplant." We sat in stunned silence as he spoke. The one surgical procedure that could fix a large, weak, tired heart was unfathomable to us.

Two years after his initial diagnosis of CHF, Miller was hospitalized at Caldwell Memorial Hospital in June with cellulites, after having cut his leg. While there, his cardiologist decided to go ahead with Miller's usual echocardiogram that was scheduled to happen in August. It came back with startling results.

Despite a five percent improvement in January 1999, he was now thirty-five percent worse. His heart was working at only fifteen percent of normal.

His old symptoms returned along with some new ones. His ankles swelled up to three times their normal size. He was nauseated and suffered from extreme shortness of breath. He lost his sense of taste and began having trouble remembering things, sometimes stopping in mid-sentence because he had forgotten what he was going to say.

Before being released from Caldwell Memorial, Miller's cardiologist had already made the appointment for Miller's heart transplant evaluation at the Sanger Clinic, the transplant center of Carolinas Medical Center in Charlotte, North Carolina.

DEATH LEADS THE WAY

The scene in the examining room at the Sanger Clinic was like a bad movie-of-the-week. The doctor was sitting on a stool, his nurse standing behind him holding a folder. Miller was on the exam table, long legs dangling, I on a chair at his feet. "I have bad news and good news," the doctor began. I looked at the nurse. She was looking at the floor. She can't look at me, I thought. This must be bad. "The bad news is that your heart is very sick and if you don't get a new heart soon you won't live another twelve months," he said. I took Miller's hand. "The good news is that we can give you a new heart." I looked at Miller and his tears matched mine.

So this is how you get a death sentence, I thought. What do you do when you find out you only have a year to live? How are you supposed to act? I don't know about you, but I've played with the idea of knowing I only had a short time to live. Usually, this thought comes about for me as a result of being a hospice volunteer or hearing that someone I know has been diagnosed with cancer. I'm not sure in those initial moments or first few days whether either Miller or I really thought about what we were going to do. So much happened at first.

Miller was so sick they admitted him into Carolinas Medical Center the same day the doctor pronounced his prognosis. And then he spent the first week being evaluated for transplant, which involves a series of tests and consultations with several specialists. Miller slept most of the time in between these tests and consults. He was very weak and many of the initial visits with the transplant nurses and the transplant social worker he slept through as I took notes to tell him about later.

But for me reality started sinking in the day Miller was admitted into the hospital and I had to go home without him. I knew once I got home I would face the hardest part, telling our children, Marson, age 18, and 16-year old Molly. I was still numb from the news; I could still hear the doctor's voice in my head as I left the hospital that afternoon to go home. To this day, I don't know how I found my car in the parking garage let alone found my way back to the highway from the hospital. Horror filled me as I drove, until the sobs broke free. It was dusk, in between the brightness of day and the bronze of twilight. I couldn't bring myself to rehearse the words I needed to say to my children.

In the driveway I sat in the dark, quiet car, listening to the silence. I would do this often in the months to follow. It would become my own version of dusk, a time in between the reality of hospitals and diagnoses and the reality of teenage angst and mounting problems. My car would become my refuge. Whether sitting in front of Carolinas Medical Center's Hospitality House in Charlotte or, later, on the fourth floor of the parking deck of The Cleveland Clinic, where our insurance company would eventually send us for the transplant, that car represented home to me. It was the only constant in my life. It smelled the same as it did before Miller got sick, was the same color, no changes. And as I sat that evening, contemplating how I would put into words this incredible truth, I knew that somewhere, whether it was in this car or inside myself, I would have to find some inner strength.

They were inside the kitchen, foraging, when I came in. "Where's Dad?" Molly asked.

"Sit down, we have to talk," I said.

I don't recall the exact words I used; I only remember talking about enlarged hearts, end-stage cardiac disease, transplants, waiting, not worrying, staying in the hospital, pulling together. I do remember watching those two fresh faces, faces with clear, trusting eyes; begin to fade in front of me. Molly's compressed into a red, wet puddle. Marson's blinked into steely silence, allowing only one tear at a time to roll out.

I laid out the plan. Our family always liked to have a plan. We would wake up on weekend mornings and someone would ask, "Okay. What's the plan for today?" Now, the plan was for me to go to Charlotte each day until Dad got out of the hospital (Lenoir is about an hour and forty-five minutes north of Charlotte), for Molly to go to school, and Marson to go to college. The plan was to keep going the way we were, only without Dad. After all, he would be home soon, right? The plan called for us to stick together, not fall apart.

ENTERING "THE WAIT"

We were living with a ticking time bomb. It hit me the day I met with the transplant social worker. Energetic and bird-like, she was a compassionate woman who understood immediately the strain I was under. At this point I felt like I was holding it together pretty well. But as I listened to her quietly and carefully explain what we were going to face in the months ahead beginning with "the Wait," I felt the first small crack.

Matching a donor to a recipient begins with blood type and body size. There is no cross matching. If you have type A blood, then you must have a type A donor. Rh factor is irrelevant, so it doesn't matter if you're positive and the donor is negative. Miller is a type O. As a universal blood donor, I thought this was a good thing, only to find out that just like the other types, a type O recipient needs a type O donor. No breaks here. Type O is also the most common blood type; therefore, type O's typically wait longer because the "competition" is higher for type O hearts. More rare blood types, such as type B, may wait a shorter amount of time.

When Miller was admitted into the hospital, he weighed about 185. This was good news for us, since his weight was compatible with receiving a man's or a woman's heart. Typically, the very large patient and the very small person will wait longer than someone of a more average size. With blood type and body weight now factored into our equation, the social worker told us our wait could be as short as three months or as long as six. But she also knew patients who had gotten a heart within a week of being listed; you just never knew what could happen.

The only thing that reassured me was when she said most of the patients get to wait at home, that only the very sickest have to spend "the Wait" in the hospital. UNOS, (United Network of Organ Sharing) the national registry of all those waiting for organ transplant, lists you by status. Status 1 patients have the highest priority since they are considered the most critical. Status 1 patients must be in the Intensive Care Unit or the Intermediate Care Unit (the Transplant Special Care Unit) on what are called intravenous inotropes, such as dobutamine, a life-sustaining drug, or other life support devices. Status 2 patients wait at home or in the hospital but not in the Intensive Care Unit. They may be treated with home dobutamine. I felt sure Miller wasn't going to be Status 1. (Oh, ignorance *is* bliss.)

I drove home from the hospital that day thinking about "the Wait." Six months still gave us plenty of time to beat the twelve-month "dead-line." I said the first of many prayers to God, asking for Miller to get a heart. Suddenly it hit me, how can I pray for someone else to die so that my husband can live? How do you pray in a situation like this? What exactly should I pray for? We can get what we need only at the expense of someone else? I couldn't stop the tears that warmed my face and eyes as I hurtled down I-77 toward home.

The next day I presented my predicament to the social worker. Her response was that we aren't praying for someone else to die so that we can have his or her organs. Destiny or God or whatever you believe in has already predetermined that the death is going to happen. The act of asking for a donor organ takes place only after the doctor declares a person legally brain-dead. Brain death is the irreversible and complete cessation of all brain and brain stem functions. It means there is no blood flow through the brain or brain stem and the patient has stopped responding to outside stimuli. She said we should pray for the family of the donor and the difficult situation they are in. In North Carolina the family becomes the legal custodian of the brain-dead loved one. They are the ones who make that all-important decision whether to donate their loved one's organs or not.

Suddenly, donors and their families became real people to me. Like shadows behind a screen, they were present. I began to pray for them. What an unbearable situation to be in at such a difficult moment in your life, I thought. After Miller's transplant I would learn from Neal Evans, a procurement coordinator for Carolina Donor Services, our region's organ procurement agency, that when a patient is brain dead, his loved ones must go through a process called "de-coupling." This is the time it takes them to separate the information that their loved one is not going to recover from their hopes for recovery. They can intellectually know that the person is not going to wake up and get well, but their emotions still hang onto a silent promise of recovery. De-coupling can take several hours or several days.

I'm not sure why, but I wish this was something I had known going in. This miraculous event of transplant, although happy in outcome for the recipient and his family, is surrounded on all sides by sorrow and grief. It is a two-sided sword, with both sides facing death. Once you are on the transplant journey, you become bound not only to other patients and their families, but also to all the donors and their families as well. You enter a private society where empathy is the ruling emotion and love is your guide. Just as we as loved ones of patients are affected by a diagnosis, so too are the loved ones of a donor affected by their loved one's trauma. The picture of organ transplant becomes wider in scope when you consider that there are so many more than just two lives caught in the net of this life-altering drama.

A Lesson In Dying

In these first moments, we must face death and make decisions based on our own feelings about death. As I drove back and forth to the hospital each day, I thought a lot about death—not just Miller's, but my own, my children's, my parents', my pets'. I remembered an exercise I did a few years ago in my hospice volunteer training. The leader of the session handed us five slips of paper and told us to write on each one the name of a person we were close to or an activity we especially liked doing. I wrote down Miller, Molly, Marson, books, and pets. Then we laid the pieces of paper down in a row in front of ourselves. She began to read a beautifully written detailed account of an unnamed person's life, sickness, and impending death. We were supposed to imagine we were that unnamed person. She read of how we had been diagnosed with a terminal illness and we had decided to die at home. She read of how we started off feeling pretty good, just a few symptoms, but how we slowly began to change. She read the changes we faced in our appearance, our feelings, and our surroundings. We went from sleeping in our own rooms to having a hospital bed put in the living room. We went from being healthy and robust to less than half our weight, with no energy. She read of our loss of bowel functioning and our inability to feed ourselves. She read about our total dependence on another person and our total release of all control we had over our life. During the reading she would stop and ask us to remove one of the pieces of paper, which she collected in a basket.

At the end of the reading, when we were left with only two pieces of paper, it began to get scary. You were choosing the things you would have to give up because you were dying and you were incapable of doing those things or being with that person. For me death became about prioritizing and about letting go. Marson was the first of my pieces to go. I figured he'd be in college anyway. The next thing to go were my books. I figured I'd probably be too sick to read anyway. The next thing to go were my pets. As much as I love my dogs, I figured I wouldn't be able to take care of them anyway.

When it got down to two pieces of paper, the leader had us turn them over and move them around until we'd forgotten which was which. She proceeded to read about the last days and hours of our life. She read in almost a whisper and walked around the room removing one piece of paper from each of us. The room was eerily quiet. Some of the participants were dabbing at tears, muffling sniffles. I was numb. This felt too real. At the moment of our death she told us to turn over the last piece of paper. Mine said Molly.

I could really feel myself transformed to my bedroom at home. Lying in my bed, covers pulled up to my chin, the time ticking away my last breaths, and there by my bed, holding my hand, was my daughter. For me, facing death became about making the most of life right now. Facing death is about facing the relationships in your life. The emotional impact this exercise had on the group was incredible. One woman jumped from her chair and ran out of the room sobbing. It is the closest thing to experiencing my own death I have ever had.

Facing death means facing the details of dying. Because Miller had never had a major illness in the eighteen years of our marriage, there was no reason for him to have a Living Will or "advanced directives." We did have regular wills, but this was different. In the event Miller was on life support, would he want to continue this or not? Who would have the decision of continuing or discontinuing life support? The hospital had a notary who could make the Living Will and his advanced directives legal. All we had to do was read it and have Miller sign it. They would take care of witnesses.

The only word I can use to describe the scene was creepy. I was sitting on Miller's hospital bed, talking to the hospital's notary public so matter-of-factly about who would pull the plug. I envisioned Miller, lying in bed, dying, with tubes everywhere and a doctor coming in to pull out a baseball-size plug in the wall as we all watched. It was horrifying. I was numb. Was this really us going through this?

It seemed like just a few months ago we had been on the golf course. I could still feel the warm breeze, smell the sweet pine needles. I could still see that white speck flying across a blue sky toward its green destination, Miller's arm around me as we bumped along the fairway in the golf cart. What had happened to our life? Where had it gone? Why was I sleeping alone and planning my husband's last moments on earth?

After it was signed, witnessed, notarized, and a copy put in the chart, I took home the Living Will to put it with the other wills. I keep our important papers in a locked, fireproof box under my bed. I held the box in my hands. I laid it on the bed. I felt like I was in a dream. I didn't want to look inside but I was drawn to the contents inside the box. The little key wouldn't work in the lock at first, but with a little pressure it turned the lock and the box popped opened. On top were the children's birth certificates, last used for Molly's registration on the school tennis team and Marson's admission to college. Underneath was Miller's life insurance policy. There was my life insurance policy. There were our wills, rubber banded together. I took them out.

It was about 10:00 at night. Marson was out; Molly was in her room on the phone. My room was quiet. I opened the plastic folder the life insurance policy was in. Death benefits. This is what I would get when Miller died. The tears dropped and slid down the plastic. It felt morbid, looking at dollar signs, thinking of how I would probably use the money to pay off our bills and move somewhere else or nowhere else. I felt ashamed for thinking he might die, a traitor. I also felt old and tired. Knowing that at some point in life, either he or I would be examining these documents, I felt like I should be in my eighties, like I was outside myself looking at myself in the very distant future.

I took his will from underneath the rubber band. It came out of its folder stiffly, having been put there some ten years ago. I remembered our going to see Rebecca, my friend since childhood who was now our attorney. I remembered sitting in her paneled office, discussing the fates of my children, should anything happen to Miller and me. That was the reason for the wills, to make sure there would be someone to take care of our children in the event we were both killed at the same time. The thought then that something would happen was remote and surreal. Wills were just an ounce of prevention, after all. You didn't really use them until you were old and you'd lived a long, full life. So why was I reading Miller's now, when he was only forty?

I squeezed my eyes tight, holding in the sob I knew was threatening to choke me if I didn't release it. Miller and I had talked briefly today about his funeral. "We have to be grown up about this," he said. No open casket, cremation instead. Memorial service? Yes. What about that AME Zion choir you loved last Christmas? Yes, that would be nice. Ashes sprinkled, no urn on the mantel.

Dropping the box on the floor, I dissolved into my tears and I could see myself in black, my children in black, the church in black with a black coffin and black flowers. I could hear the AME Zion choir. The music was haunting, the choir members were black, and their robes were black. They were crying as I was crying. "God, oh Heavenly Father," I prayed, "please don't let him die."

PRAYING FOR MIRACLES

The God I believe in is a loving being and all love comes from Him. I believe he gave each one of us free will and we all have choices and must live with the results of those choices. This is why I could never blame God for Miller's predicament.

God did not make Miller sick. Miller's physiology is what made him sick. God was not punishing Miller, our children, or me.

I've always felt a strong connection to my God. I was baptized and confirmed in the Episcopal Church and first learned about God through Sunday school and the Book of Common Prayer. I remember when I was a little girl, coming home from Sunday School after learning the creation story and looking around my backyard in awe, thinking "God made all this."

When I was thirteen, I was told my mother might have a brain tumor. I don't know how I found out about it, but a neighbor down the street held a prayer meeting every Tuesday night. So, during that time, I would walk to her house on Tuesday nights and have those attending pray for my mother. As it turned out, my mother didn't have a brain tumor and that was the beginning of what has evolved into a long, comforting prayer life.

At 21, I was single, living alone in Charlotte, where I had been transferred just a few months before. I was unhappy with the move. The work and people weren't what I'd expected. I missed my family and friends. I tried to make the best of things, but once after an unusually bad day I came home very depressed. I began to cry and soon the sobs were gut-wrenching as I pleaded with God to help get me out of this horrible situation. Knowing that another transfer was impossible, I went to work the next day thinking that it was in God's hands now. There was nothing left to do but endure. My manager came up to me soon I after I got there and told me the district manager wanted to know if I'd be interested in moving again, even though I had just moved! I jumped at the chance and ended up in a smaller town and friendlier situation that eventually brought me back to my hometown, where I met Miller again after four years of being away. And the rest, as they say, is history.

Since then, I have watched the power of prayer work over and over again in my life. I believe that this intimate conversation with God has the power to transform you and those you pray for. Even scientists are now admitting there's something to it. In 1998, Duke University researchers proved that the recovery of surgical patients (findings were based on cardiac surgery patients) could be from 50 to 100 percent better if someone prayed for them.

Needless to say, from the very beginning, I made sure Miller was on every prayer list I could find. I called our local parish, I called our hometown parish, and I approached complete strangers. One time, about three months into our wait, I was at an Ohio Wal-Mart and stopped to buy baked goods from a church youth group who had set up a table in front of the store. They were ecstatic to see how much I was buying, so I explained how I was buying the cakes for the folks I was staying with and the cookies for the guys in the hospital. I told them about Miller and the other people at the Transplant Special Care Unit waiting to have organ transplants. They sat silently listening. One of the girls took out a piece of paper and a pen and asked me to print Miller's name on it. She explained that her church had a special intercessional prayer group and she would add Miller's name to the list of those they prayed for each week. The other kids joined in with their own promises to pray for Miller and the other patients. I was touched by their sincerity.

My philosophy became, and still is, you can never have too many people praying. Whenever people asked if there was anything they could do, I would always ask them to pray for Miller and add him to their church's prayer list. To this day, I believe that is why Miller's recovery has been so phenomenal.

FOLLOWING THE GOD OF HOPE

In a town as small as Lenoir, where you're thirty minutes from the nearest big town, it's impossible to find anyone else whose husband is waiting for a heart transplant. Since our hospital was in another state, there were no family support groups I could attend locally and since I visited the Cleveland Clinic on weekends, their support groups weren't meeting when I was there. It was hard to explain to people what I was going through, so I stopped trying.

During the months that followed Miller's admission into the Clinic, my children were involved with their friends and I began to spend many nights at home alone. For comfort, I meditated and prayed. My prayers turned into mini-conversations with God, telling Him my feelings, my fears, sometimes I wept. He became my best friend. I could feel His presence in my room or the car or the front stoop. At night I'd fall asleep with my head on my pillow, envisioning my head on His lap and Him smoothing my hair. This was enormously comforting.

I turned to my prayer book. I started reading the Morning Prayer and Evening Prayer services each day. One day, a particular verse of scripture jumped out at me. *May the God of hope fill us with all joy and peace in believing through the power of the Holy Spirit, Romans 15:13.* The God of hope...yes, that is what He had become for me. Our relationship had transformed from my always asking for help to my leaning on Him daily, deriving all my hope for my future and Miller's future from His presence.

I knew I had to make a conscious decision every day to let go of Miller and all my worries. Like taking off a heavy wool sweater that's been drenched by rain, I handed my life, a wet, soggy mess, to Him. I knew that I was truly not alone on my journey. God was in control and He had a plan. I was just along for the ride. After all, hadn't He arranged for Miller to have tests earlier than he was to? At the rate Miller had been declining when he went into the hospital in June, what would have happened if he had waited until August to have that echocardiogram? Hadn't God led us to the number one heart center in the nation? Hadn't He provided me with everything I needed since this whole thing began? I knew then He had always provided everything I needed my whole life and He would not turn His back on me now.

I opened my Bible, and the words of Psalm 121 jumped off the page. *"I will Lift up mine eyes unto the hills. From whence cometh my help? My help cometh from the Lord, who made heaven and earth,"* I read aloud. Thousands of years ago the person who wrote those words was looking out at the hills and mountains as I was, suffering and wondering how he would survive his crisis. And God had come to him as He came to me. Human suffering has gone on for centuries and it will continue for centuries to come. All we have to sustain us through our suffering is the solace that we are not alone and that God suffers along with us.

Miller and I had every reason to hope. According to our cardiologist, 95 percent of patients survive heart transplant surgery. And, deaths from rejection are uncommon. Once the wait was over, Miller could look forward to many years of health.

Waiting

Waiting tastes like lukewarm coffee.
Waiting feels like friction
between rough hands
around hot Styrofoam.

Waiting sounds like a humming clock.
And a foot and finger
keeping time with time.
Sirens, crickets
and the hiss and bubble
of a coffee maker.

Waiting smells of new earth
and diesel fuel,
white cafeteria food,
and burnt charcoal
at the bottom of the pot.

Waiting is a stubborn child,
a rock,
refusing to negotiate.
Waiting is a jailer,
who taps my shoulder,
and then silently
locks the cuffs.

Seven ceiling tiles across,
seven ceiling tiles from foot to head,
all above a field of flecks,
blue carpet with 300 red specks,
too many beige freckles on white linoleum.
Waiting calls me to account.

Waiting, be kind to me.
Be merciful and set me free.
You stand in the door, waiting,
waiting for word to let me be.

2

"Waiting is the hardest part."

—Tom Petty

LIFE IN LIMBO

In the world of organ transplants, the United Network of Organ Sharing, UNOS, list of those in need takes on a magical quality equal to that of Willy Wonka's golden ticket. It's your pass to another chance, a shiny strand of hope that will pull you safely onboard life again.

"The List" is the only fair and equitable way to distribute organs. Without it, many would die who could have been saved. Once a healthy organ becomes available the donor's hospital contacts UNOS, who accesses the list of possible recipients. A candidate is chosen after each possible recipient is measured against specific criteria for matching, including their locality, blood type, body size, severity of condition, and length of time waiting. It doesn't matter who you are, how much money you have, what color or sex you are, to "the List" you are a mixture of components that will make you eligible or not. It doesn't play favorites and everyone gets a chance.

Once Miller joined the ranks of those on "the List," we soon learned the truth; rocker Tom Petty's song was right—waiting *is* the hardest part. The average wait for heart transplant patients is three to six months. It's a wait built on uncertainty. We met people who would end up waiting eight or nine months. We even heard about a man in another hospital that waited a year. We met a man who came in on Monday and was transplanted on Friday. And we met the ones that wouldn't make it.

At first, it's not so bad. The beginning of the wait is full of false hope that you will be the exception to the rule. There's no way, I thought, we will have to wait as long as everyone else. But as the weeks went by, I realized we weren't the chosen ones. We were going to have to wait just like everyone else and there was no way around it. This was not a wait you could hurry. The time getting ready for the wait had flown by. Now we were in it and the door behind us was shut and locked. There was only one thing to do…be patient…be a patient…wait.

FAMILY FALLING THROUGH THE CRACKS

But, during the wait, there is one certainty: it will affect everyone in your family. We would all enter into our own worlds of suffering. For me, it was the most horrible experience I have ever had to endure; yet it also became the most spiritually renewing and personally empowering experience I've ever been blessed with. But it took a while to get to that place.

My children felt lost and left out. They dealt with it by acting out in all kinds of ways. Marson lost all interest in college and called me, begging to come home. Twice I visited him at school and saw the tears in his I eyes as he explained how guilty he felt for being there instead of at home helping me. I wanted so much for him to have the "college experience," going to classes, hanging out with friends in dorm rooms and coffee houses talking about the "deeper meaning" of life. I wanted him to discover new things and find something he loved to do. But most of all I wanted him to be happy. But he kept saying, "Mom, I need to be helping you."

Marson and I have always been close. He loves the things I love: writing, reading, and cooking. He's quiet and plays his guitar and writes his own songs. He's always been a good kid. Sure he'd had his moments in high school, just like any other kid, but at eighteen he was a caring individual who was pleasant company. I love him so much and really battled with myself about what was best for him. The last thing I wanted was to force him to do something he didn't want to do. But I really felt like he needed to be away from all the heavy stuff at home. Maybe I was trying to protect him; maybe I was trying to be too strong. Over and over I would try to convince him to hang in there.

It was Parent's Day at Warren Wilson College and I had just said good-bye to my son as he left with three of his friends. We had agreed to meet back at his room after I had visited with a few of his professors. It was early fall and the leaves had begun to turn on the campus. Situated in Swannanoa, just minutes outside of Asheville, North Caroline, the Warren Wilson campus is a working farm with the epicenter composed of beautiful rock buildings and centuries-old trees.

As I walked along the drive I saw Marson's dorm manager. When I introduced myself to him he began to tell me some startling facts about my son. Marson had confided in this man about his father's situation and he felt I should know how depressed Marson had become. The man told me he felt Marson should go home until the transplant happened. I thanked him for the information and with a heavy heart continued on my way to meet with Marson's dean.

She was a striking woman, with dark brown eyes. We sat in her office and she proceeded to reiterate what the dorm manager had told me. Finally she said to me, "Mrs. Nance, sometimes we can be too strong, shutting out the people who want to be strong for us. You need your son with you, at home, now. He is always welcome to come back."

She was right. In my effort to hold things together for my children, and myself, I was trying to make them fit into a mold that wasn't right for them. I did need them with me.

I was glad to have him home. For one thing he had been working in our pawn shop since he was fourteen and knew a lot more than I did about how things worked there. Also, it was nice having a guy, and usually a couple of his friends, at the house at night. I felt safer being out in the country with him home. But most of all, I felt like one of the missing puzzle pieces was back in place where it belonged. Now my family was missing only one piece.

Molly on the other hand, proved to be a lot more difficult during this time. She acted out in a variety of ways including skipping school and lying to me. I think part of this was a normal teenager taking advantage of her mother being out of town and part was her fear of losing Miller. She is a beautiful girl, full of life and laughter. It hurt me to see her becoming a surly, angry teenager.

"It's too depressing around here!" she would exclaim, time and time again. She found refuge in the home of a friend, a "normal" family, as she put it. I was so grateful to that family for treating her as one of their own and giving her a place to escape the turmoil of her own family, but at the same time, I felt hurt that she didn't want to be with me.

Once again, I was torn: should I stay home with her more and visit Miller less? Should I take her with me every time I went to Cleveland even though her school was holding her to their attendance policy? I went to the school and spoke with each teacher. I asked if they could give Molly assignments in advance to take with her. Most of her teachers didn't make lesson plans that far in advance. They suggested she attend the make-up classes when she got back.

Every time Molly went with me to Cleveland she missed two days of classes. This meant that for every trip she would need eight hours of make-up time. Make-up days were on Tuesday and Thursday from 3:00 p.m. to 5:00 p.m.; Molly would be able to make up only one class per make-up day. It would take her four weeks to make up one trip with me. By the end of the semester, I had to go to the school and talk to the teachers about "forgiving" some of the absences because there wasn't enough time to make them all up. It was frustrating for me and for Molly it felt like punishment, making her dig her heels in more and beg to be left at home.

As for myself, unfortunately, I've made it a habit throughout my life to isolate myself when bad things happen. I've always liked solitude, it gives me a time and safe place to think things out, but in this case my isolationist tendencies worked against me. As far as my fellow church members were concerned, once they stopped seeing me on Sundays, they assumed I had moved to Cleveland or that I didn't want to be bothered. I didn't hear from them. I think most people just didn't know what to say to me. It made them uncomfortable and like I said before, if you appear to be strong and getting along okay, I think most people assume you are.

As I withdrew more and more into my own world, which was hurtling along at a jetliner's pace, it never occurred to me that I was the one who was supposed to reach out. After the transplant, when I talked to people who had no idea what had happened to my family, there was one friend in particular who blasted me for not calling her. I realized then that reaching out to others works like a news service. Sometimes the only way they're going to get the news is if you tell them. And if you don't tell them, you deprive them of helping you, which in turn helps them cope with the situation.

If I had it to do over again, I would force myself to seek out more support. I would make myself go to church suppers and Sunday school. I would make myself call a friend at least once a week for lunch. I would start with "A" in my address book and call everyone in it, not to complain about my situation, but to give me and those people in the address book a chance to connect. After all, it's not every day someone you know goes into the hospital for a heart transplant. There's not a Hallmark card for this one. And it's easy to get caught up in the patient's life and death drama and forget there's a family somewhere behind the scenes trying to carry on.

WAIT WITH A CAPITAL "W"

According to UNOS, there are now (in October, 2003) over eighty thousand patients waiting for organ transplants. To me this means there are also at least that many people waiting alongside those patients. These are people, like me, whose lives will be altered by the effects of their loved one's transplant experience. Our lives are lived in limbo, purgatory on earth, trying to get through the day-to-day routines with a huge question hanging above: will he/she make it another day without a donor?

There's no fairness in the wait. In her book *Ready, Set, Wait…Help for Life on Hold*, Karen Barber talks about how waiting goes "beyond the fairness rules." According to Barber, "Our wagons are bound to break down irreparably when we treat gigantic life quests like the post office line where fairness rules apply…Unfortunately, in the Wait our turn at life's window may not come today. Nor tomorrow. In fact, it may never come, even though we have been waiting a very long time, much longer than others already served. We cannot estimate durations by how fast the line is moving; we cannot rank order by arrival time; we cannot expect that line crashers will be censored. No amount of fill in activities, timetable planning, preparation, or patience will satisfy such inequities."

The only thing you can do is live with and deal with each day (and night) as it comes. In my case it was unproductive to blame Miller for this situation. It was exhausting to try to live into what other people thought I should do. And it was unreasonable to feel guilty. Being told to be patient was like salt in a wound: it didn't make it feel any better. I was just along for the ride and I just had to maintain.

When you enter the big wait, "with a capital W," as Barber calls it, all the little waits that used to be so irritating suddenly don't bother you as much. I used to be one of the complainers when I went to K-Mart and saw that out of their two dozen cash registers they had only two open. Now, it didn't matter. Where did I have to rush off to? Waiting in line at K-Mart was a piece of cake compared to the wait I was in. The line actually moved.

One day I was coming home from a visit with my parents when I decided to stop at a fast food restaurant for a drink and bathroom break. The place was deserted except for one very large woman standing at the counter. There was a young black man working the register and it appeared he was also doing the cooking and manning the drive-thru. I went to the restroom and when I came out the woman was still waiting and the young man was hurriedly trying to fill a drive-thru order. The woman was obviously upset, complete with heaving sighs and a chilly stare at me when I got in line behind her. When he finally asked her for her order she was very rude, saying something about it's taking so long. I could tell the young man was working as hard as he could and I wanted to tell this woman, "Hey, what's your hurry? What's a little wait in the grand scheme of waiting? Isn't life one big wait, after all?" But I kept my mouth shut and tried to be especially nice to the poor guy stuck with this crummy situation.

In January, Miller and I were at the vending machines in, ironically, the out-patient surgery building. It was about 7:00 p.m. We were trying to get our dollar bill to go into a drink machine that didn't want it when a young woman came in. She was pacing and sighing (that should have tipped us off) and grumbling. You could tell she wanted to tell us something. Suddenly she burst out, "I've been waiting in this hospital since 9:00 this morning."

Without missing a beat, Miller spoke up, "Yeah? Well I've been here since August." The woman's eyes almost popped out of her head and she turned and hurried out. No sympathy here.

I turned to Miller and said, "Boy, did she complain to the wrong person." We started laughing. Waiting really is just a state of mind.

For Miller, it was a time of constant wondering. "I saw so many people come and go, being transplanted or not making it. I was always wondering when my time would come, when I would get my transplant. I tried not to think about if it wouldn't happen, but it's hard not to, especially as I felt myself getting weaker. I knew I had to make it; I had so much to live for, so I held onto the faith that I would get home to my family."

IN FOR THE DURATION

So, I joined the thousands of brave individuals who choose to stay and face the fear alongside their loved ones. Yes, I said choose to stay. I did have a choice. During Miller's initial evaluation, one of the things the transplant team looks at is what kind of family support the patient has. I was surprised to learn that in some cases, spouses will leave when confronted with the reality of organ transplant. Depending on an individual's insurance coverage, it can be financially draining, not just the transplant procedure itself, but the lifetime of prescription drugs a patient will take. The emotional toll it takes on everyone involved is enough to scare even the most dedicated. The social worker explained that some times when these terms are spelled out and you realize that once you're in, there's no turning back, some make the decision not to participate.

But I really and truly believed in the "sickness and health" part of our wedding vows. I was committed to Miller and to what we had together. I would not run out on him. If I was to stay for the duration, I had to be willing to sacrifice the comfort level of the ordinariness of my life to step into this extraordinary situation. To survive the wait I had to develop a new kind of strength, determination and faith. It was a conscious decision that anyone faced with any kind of hardship can make. And in a real sense, that is what this book is really about. Strength, determination, and faith don't have to be staunch words that involve incredible sacrifice and fear. It is in the little things that we find the greatest sources of these three important traits. It started with fixing my gaze forward, even when my confidence was shaky, and holding tightly to a deep belief that Miller and I would make it on this long journey back to life.

I Miss You

I miss you.
There, I've said it
and now like a boil lanced
the black hurt can ooze out.

But that's not enough.
Missing you is not enough.
I miss you,
but mostly I miss
who I was
when I was with you.

And what we had,
what we lost,
what we were working on.

I miss the strength you gave me
like the walking stick you gave me
with its special carved places
the exact size of my hand.

I miss the comfort of your arms
and of running my fingers
through your chest hair
as I run my fingers now
through the blades of grass
on our front lawn.

I miss the laughter and joy
and secrets
and promises
and normalcy.

I miss you.

3

"What doesn't kill you makes you stronger."

—Unknown

A TRAIL OF TRIALS

Everything is going along smoothly in your life. You make plans; you set goals; you look to the future with hope. The bad things in life are all in the news and you wrap yourself in a blanket woven of the secure repetition and expectancy of your days, comforted by the fact that you are safe from the bad things. Then one day you wake up and, poof! Something has come along while you were looking the other way and stripped you of your security blanket. The bad thing has forced the denial from your mind and you must stare squarely at your worst-case scenario. That's the way it happened for me. Like a cruel magic trick, now you see it, now you don't. My world was rocked to its very core. I was alone in a life that demanded dual participation. I was faced with filling my role and Miller's role in my life.

How do you cope with suddenly being thrust into someone else's responsibilities? Miller and I had created a marriage where he had responsibilities, I had responsibilities and we had shared responsibilities. Basically, I stayed out of running the pawnshop. I made the bank deposits and paid the bills. He took care of making loans, purchasing merchandise, making deals. And he stayed out of the copywriting business, except to tell me I wasn't charging enough. Together, we decided what was best for our children and how to spend our money. With him out of the picture, I didn't have his 25-plus years of experience to fall back on and no one else in the shop did either.

I felt solely responsible for the pawnshop. My goal became simply to maintain things until Miller returned. I would be satisfied with having the shop still here with money still in the bank by the time Miller got back.

Thankfully, I did have Miller's cousin, Lewis, our business partner, who had also been raised by a pawnbroker, and he was soon to become one of my knights in shining armor. He lived in our hometown of Fayetteville, about a four-hour drive to Lenoir. But I could ask him to leave his wife and year-old baby to come to Lenoir to my rescue only so many times. I felt guilty for asking, although he was always ready and willing to come help.

STRESS: THE SILENT STALKER

I was under a lot of stress. And the strange thing about stress is how incredibly sneaky it is. You don't wake up one morning and say, "Boy this stress is killing me." Stress takes time to build up. It silently gnaws at you as you're faced with decisions and situations each day and you attempt to deal with each one.

In a normal day, situations and challenges come at me with big gaps in between. There may a difficult problem to solve, but there's enough time before I have to face the next problem to take a breath and figure out what I'm going to do. In my new situation, the decisions and challenges came at me like bullets from an automatic pistol. I didn't have time to figure the first thing out before the next thing happened. There were decisions to be made at the hospital that directly affected me, such as whether Miller should accept a heart from a donor with Hepatitis C or not. There were decisions to be made at the pawnshop, such as whether to hire someone to fill in for Miller or not. There were decisions to be made about my children, such as taking Marson out of college or not or taking Molly to Cleveland or not. There were decisions about my work, to continue it or not, and there were decisions about my pets, who would take care of my four dogs while I was gone? The tension got higher and higher each day. The yard needed mowing, the filter in the well needed changing, the trash needed to be taken to the dump. Should Miller participate in a drug study? Would Molly resent going to a counselor? Would Marson ever go back to college? I felt like my skull would explode. The stress had suddenly come out of hiding and demanded to be a presence in my life.

I really began to feel it as it began to rob me of things. One of the first casualties of my stress was my concentration. Reading has always been one of my biggest pleasures. I have been known to wake up on a Sunday morning and sit down and not get up until I have read a book from cover to cover. Suddenly, I couldn't read a magazine article and remember what I'd read. My well-trained eyes did what they were supposed to do, back and forth, back and forth across the page. But my brain refused to listen. It had its own agenda. It was working on problems. As hard as I tried, I could not read or enjoy reading any more.

The worst part of this was that my copywriting business involved lots of reading. Not just reading, but delving into a client's product, learning what it did if I didn't know and then figuring out why anyone would buy it. To write effective, persuasive advertising copy, you have to understand the product, the person buying it, and the motivations behind his decision to buy it. Then you have to turn the answers to those issues into clever, quick, concise sentences because there's not a lot of room on an 8 ½" by 11" piece of paper, the size of a 3-panel brochure. Space is always limited and there's always a lot to say. I might be working with a ¼" ad or a 15 second radio spot. Every word becomes important when you only have enough space for a three-word headline. And of course they were paying for creativity. Just any words wouldn't do.

Inevitably, the second casualty of my stress was my business. Besides not being able to concentrate long enough to read, I could not work at the pawnshop, visit Miller every other weekend, and maintain quality work for my copywriting clients, which included keeping their deadlines. Advertising is all about deadlines. Plain and simple. When the account executive promises the client copy on a certain day, the copywriter better have it or can forget about ever working for them again. Hey, I wouldn't want to be them in a meeting, facing their client who's about to spend the big bucks on an idea, from which my pay would come, without the thing I'd promised. It could get ugly and you, the account exec, would be out on the street. In all the years I'd been copywriting, I was proud of the fact that I'd never missed a deadline. Dependability was one of the things that separated me from my competition. I always came through. That's why I cut my losses before I had any. When I had a lull between jobs, I called my clients and told them it was time for me to take a hiatus. Everyone understood and told me to call as soon as Miller was okay and I could resume working.

I had been a copywriter for almost ten years. It would be strange not to have a project twirling in my head or to play with words for headlines. I spent so much of my time thinking, researching, and writing ads, brochures, press kits, radio spots, and other projects, not to mention the meetings and phone calls and interviews, I wasn't sure what to do with myself at first. I was used to concrete deadlines, not an intangible one like the kind I lived with now.

I was also concerned with the loss of income when the copywriting business shut down. For the first time in years, with only my salary from the pawnshop, we were now a one-paycheck family. At the same time, the first hospital bills began coming in. In order to afford private insurance, we have a deductible we have to meet before the insurance kicks in. I became expert at negotiating payment plans with the hospitals, ambulance service, and the folks who billed us for the jet ride to Cleveland. But God always provides if we simply ask Him for what we need and then trust that He'll come through. Throughout the months, I would be given financial support from family members as well as the community.

As an aside, I did take one job well into Miller's wait. Unfortunately, it turned out the way I had feared all along, resulting in my first missed deadline. I almost lost more than a client; I almost lost a friend on that one. The lesson learned is that even when you think you have the stress under control, always assume you don't. Listen to your gut feeling when you make your decisions and stick to them. Stress is sneaky. It can hide under feelings of control. I now know I have to be careful about trusting my feelings in difficult times.

The third thing to fall victim to my stress was my confidence. Stress has an uncanny way of killing your confidence because you have all these decisions to make and problems to solve coming at you so fast and furious you are bound to make a few mistakes. But instead of sloughing them off and correcting your errors, you really let the mistakes get to you. I got to where I didn't trust myself to pick out toilet paper at the grocery store. Every decision became a big deal. Scented or unscented? Double rolls or single rolls? The 12-pack for this or the 24-pack for that? Coupon or no coupon? Name brand or store brand? I finally decided from now on it would be the white, 24-pack, single roll, unscented store brand. There, no more decision on that forever. I felt like I couldn't make a mistake with any decision, big or small. It was absurd; it was horrible.

And, like a silent stalker, the stress I was under finally manifested itself physically. I began to lose handfuls of my hair. I developed a strange sore in the middle of my tongue that would not go away. It was like a mutant taste bud, getting larger and larger, rubbing the roof of my mouth and making the sides of my tongue sore to the touch. I went to the doctor and was told it was a virus caused by stress. The doctor prescribed a mouthwash called "Magical Mouthwash." I used it several times a day, but the sore stayed with me until after the transplant. Also, my eyesight got worse, another result of stress according to my eye doctor. Even though I told myself I was doing okay, my body knew different.

LIVING WITH LOSS

The losses in my life just seemed to keep piling up. Loss of Miller, loss of copy-writing, loss of confidence, loss of security...I just wanted my life back. I would sit alone on my front steps, looking at the outline of the mountains, wondering where my life had gone. I used to have it made...up at 6:30, feed the dogs, sit on the patio on summer mornings or in front of the fire in my home office in the winter, sipping coffee, reading, Miller to work, the kids to school. I'd sit down at the computer around 9:00, my dog at my feet, my desk facing the mountains and my bird feeder, write until noon, make lunch, watch soaps, write until 4:00 or 5:00, make dinner, everyone around the table, eating, talking, watch TV or read, go to bed.

Some days I would have a meeting and I would put on my "business" clothes, drive to the big city (Greensboro, Winston-Salem, or Charlotte), meet in a pol-ished conference room with guys with ponytails and women with thick day-plan-ners, eat lunch at cute, trendy restaurants, hit a few specialty shops and come home. I loved my life as a freelance copywriter. It was who I was, so what was I supposed to do now?

Suddenly my life was about how to get Miller out of jury duty, how to fix the golf cart the kids had run into a ditch one weekend while I was in Cleveland, should I hire another person at the pawn shop or not, finding somewhere for Molly to stay so she wouldn't miss school when I visited Miller, how to pay for the medical bills that weren't covered by our insurance, how to keep Miller's '68 Firebird's battery charged, getting someone to fix the dryer, how to get the trash to the dump without a truck, how to convince Marson to stay in college, how to be strong. There were no relaxing moments sipping coffee in the morning any more. My head spun with all the things I had to do, all the things I wanted to do, things doctors and nurses had told me, and, worst of all, the memories of eigh-teen years with Miller and what life would be like without him.

I missed him with my whole self. My body missed his. My faced missed his kisses; my fingers missed his fingers intertwined with mine. The back of my neck missed the warmth of his breath softly blowing as he slept. My shoulders missed the pressure of his arms encircling them. My mind missed his quirky remarks and what in our family we refer to as "Millerisms," phrases he had made up. When he was really hungry he could "eat like a Roman" or "mill out." A good day was "a blue bird day," and something could be stuck like "a hair in a biscuit." My spirit missed his encouragement and unconditional understanding. When I would obsess about something I'd done or something someone else had done, he would tell me, "Don't worry about it. There's no future living in the past." He was my soul mate and, in all our years together I never doubted I was his.

Now, not only was he gone physically from my life, when we were together, I noticed how he had changed in appearance as well. I missed his robust 185-190 pounds of round, softness. Now he was all angles and edges at only 150 pounds. His six-foot frame was that of a skeleton, complete with bony knees, elbows and ankles. His face seemed longer and his hands had spikes for fingers. Miller lost so much weight in his fingers that the wedding band that had never been off his finger since I slipped it on eighteen years ago, now slid off easily. He kept wrapping tape around it until the tape was thick and rough. When it finally started rubbing his palm raw, he gave it to me for safekeeping. I put it on a chain and wore it around my neck. Sometimes in my most desperate bouts of missing him, I would touch it and rub it gently against my throat. The soft gold, worn smooth from years of revolving around Miller's finger, reminded me that he was never far from me.

Miller was my rock. He was steady and sure, always going to work, allowing me to go off to meetings or stay home and write all day. He asked my opinion and our marriage was a never-ending conversation. We'd always preferred each other's company to that of friends, choosing to sit off to the side at parties, talking to one another. He knew my deepest secrets and darkest fears. I knew his secret sorrows and greatest desires. I admired his musical ability; he respected my need for quiet hours to read. He was the champion of my hopes and dreams. I missed so much about our life together it felt like my insides were shattering, crumbling around my feet. My soul pined for him and what we had, stretching all the way to Ohio, with an intensity I have never felt before.

One of the things I came to miss most was his always wondering where I was and what I was doing. For years, Miller had spent all day, almost every day, at the pawnshop. I, on the other hand, had always been free to roam and would joke that Miller lived vicariously through me because he would call me so many times during the day in some of the most unexpected places. He could always track me down. I've been standing in a department store and heard the phone by the cash register ring, only to have the sales lady tell me, "It's for you." Waiting to get my oil changed, in the doctor's office, at friends' homes, at meetings, it didn't matter where I was, I could always count on Miller to wonder where I was and what I was doing. With him gone, suddenly I didn't have anyone wondering about me. The invisible cord that tied us together was cut, and I was adrift in the world. I began to tell Harry, one of the men who works for us, when I left the shop for the day, where I was going and when I would be home. He finally said to me one day, "Lisa, you don't have to tell me where you're going." I stopped dead in my tracks. The only thing I could think to say was, "But, Harry, if I don't tell someone where I am, no one will know where I am." That's when it hit me. We all need someone to wonder where we are.

Once again I would call on Psalm 121, holding on to the words at the end, which said, *"The lord shall preserve thy going out and thy coming in from this time forth and even for evermore."* Whenever I read these words, I knew I was no longer adrift in the world. There *was* someone wondering where I was and what I was doing, someone who cared about me. And in those instances I new that no matter what happened, I would be all right.

COMING TO CLEVELAND

Without a doubt, the hardest part of my situation was leaving Miller in Cleveland. It is a cruel fact of life that unless you are very wealthy, you're healthcare will be regulated by the kind of health insurance coverage you have. When we first got our health insurance policy, it never occurred to us that Miller would need a heart transplant. And as a resident of a state with five transplant centers, including Duke University Medical Center, we never would have thought it possible that we wouldn't be able to have such a procedure right here in our home state. Unfortunately for us, our insurance company did not have a contract with any of the transplant centers in North Carolina. Instead, we would have to go to one they did have one with. In our case it was the Cleveland Clinic Foundation, in Cleveland, Ohio.

I saw the trauma team, two women and three men dressed in royal blue coveralls, working quickly around Miller as I entered his room in the ICU. Breathless from rushing through the large hospital and across the parking lot to the Charlotte Hospitality House, where I had spent the last two nights, I was relieved of my bags by one of the team members. "We'll leave in about ten minutes," he said, smiling at me.

I took Miller's hand while the other members of the team unhooked Miller from the monitors and machines on the wall behind his bed and hooked him up to portable battery-powered units. After transporting him to a gurney, we were off to the Emergency Department.

Three team members would accompany Miller and me to Cleveland. The other two would go as far as the Charlotte airport. It was the first time I had ever been in the cab of an ambulance before. Within minutes the team was lifting

Miller out of the ambulance and into the waiting Lear jet. I was the last to get on as one of the pilots directed me to sit in the back beside a tiny window. I swear the interior of that plane wasn't any bigger than the inside of my Buick.

It usually takes two and a half hours to fly to Cleveland from Charlotte. This night it took only an hour. We arrived around eleven and I was taken aback by the huge gusts of wind coming across Lake Erie when I descended from the jet. Another ambulance took us to the Clinic, where Miller and I were to learn that we had just arrived at the number one heart center in America.

When we arrived, we knew nothing about the reputation of The Cleveland Clinic Foundation. The walk from the Emergency Department to the "G" Building, where Miller would live until his transplant, took us about ten minutes and led us over some of Cleveland's busiest streets. The hospital takes up about eighteen city blocks and is connected by skywalks. A person can walk miles inside this hospital without ever leaving the building. Hanging on several walls were giant banners proclaiming The Cleveland Clinic's Heart Center had been ranked number one for five years in a row by U.S. News & World Report.

I stayed with Miller in Cleveland for nine days. I didn't want to leave him but duty called back in Lenoir and staying at a hotel for that long was something I couldn't afford. I left him in the capable hands of two transplant teams, a full staff of nurses and patient care technicians, and a kindly roommate, Jack, who had been waiting for his turn at a new heart for three months.

We agreed I would visit every other weekend. I would call the social worker on the transplant team and find out about available housing. I would take care of the pawnshop, my copywriting business, the children, the dogs, and the bills. I would send Miller some civilian clothes as soon as I got home, since Jack said only the "rookies" wore their pajamas around on the floor. I was ready, yet not willing, to leave him and begin our new life.

Every other Friday, it would take me about eight hours to get to The Cleveland Clinic. I left my house at 6:00 a.m. and arrived at the hospital at about 2:00 p.m. I would leave on Monday morning. Sunday night became our time to say good-bye. At 10:00 p.m., Leo, one of the nurses who worked the nightshift, would come on the intercom and tell everyone visiting hours were over. Because all the nurses knew how far I'd come and that I was leaving the next day, they wouldn't say anything if I wanted to stay longer. But eventually, I would have to leave and Miller would walk me down to the front entrance of the hospital. We would stand in that pocket of a place, just outside the hospital lobby but not outside in the air. Because he wasn't allowed to go outside, this was as far as Miller could go. We would hold each other, Miller's IV pole pushed off to the side like an observant bystander. Like tearing little flakes of skin off a leg that's peeling from sunburn, we would let go of one another a little at a time. Whispered words of love mixed with tears accompanied words of hope. We would tell each other that the next visit would be "the big one," when Miller would get his new heart. Finally, I would turn and go through the automatic doors, back into the "real" world once again. I never looked back. I couldn't. To look back at him standing there, this shadow of the man I knew, attached from his heart to a bag on a pole by a clear, thin tube, to see him watching me leave, would mean facing what I was leaving and the pull back to him would be just too hard for me to resist. I never walked from the hospital to the parking deck across the street with clear vision.

LOOKING AT LOSS

I remember one of the first questions posed during my hospice training sessions was how do you deal with losses, any losses? Are you upset and do you agonize over the loss of your house keys or glasses? Do you get angry or frustrated when you misplace a laundry ticket or a library book? Do you become deeply depressed when a friend moves away? The leader that day told us that how you deal with the everyday losses of your life is a pretty good indication of how you will deal with the loss of a loved one. For me, it was unnerving to lose my house keys and especially my glasses, since I can't read without them. I would become frantic, interrogating everyone two or three times. And I wouldn't give up the search until the lost item was found. But I wasn't prepared for the intensity or quantity of the feelings that bubbled to the surface over the losses I was experiencing now.

Like the thick, rancid burps in a boiling cauldron, my feelings bubbled up for air. Sorrow, hopelessness, fear, paranoia, and anger. Yes, anger. I was angry at Miller for getting sick and leaving me with all this. I was sad, depressed, and lonely. I knew I needed to do something or talk to someone. I headed for my church. It was in a conversation with my minister that I first realized how abandoned I felt, and with that came grieving over the loss of the way things used to be. It helped to have someone tell me all my feelings were normal. I was especially bothered by my anger. It was interfering with my other emotions. The minister told me I was grieving. Grieving for all my losses, just as I would have grieved over the loss of a person. And anger was one of the necessary stages you have to experience to work through your grief.

Only my life had a hard-to-swallow component. I was in limbo. I couldn't just deal with my losses and move on. Yet, the experience was similar in many ways to losing a loved one. According to Elisabeth Kübler-Ross, author of *On Death and Dying,* there are four stages you must experience in order to reach full acceptance of the death of a loved one: denial and isolation; anger; bargaining; depression; and finally, acceptance. And these stages don't necessarily have to come in that order. All my losses were a result of one major loss, the loss of my husband to his disease and his move to Cleveland. I would go through these stages, and not in any order. There was no escaping them. Understanding this did not make things better, it just helped explain why I was reacting the way I was and what I could expect.

My loss was also similar to a death in the family in that after people first find out, they are interested and caring. But after about two weeks, when the dust has settled and you're supposed to be dealing with your loss and moving on, people stop calling. When Miller first went into the hospital, I would get home and there would be ten or twelve messages on the answering machine. One day there were a whopping 27 messages! Family and friends frantically called to find out how he was, if he would have to go to Cleveland, what they could do to help. By week four of his hospitalization there were no messages; life was back to normal. And I can't blame them. We all lead lives so hectic we can barely remember our own names. We all have families and bills and hassles. Life goes by so quickly, you lose track of time. Rationally, I knew all this; emotionally, I felt abandoned and alone.

Without realizing it, the kids and I talked to each other les and less about Miller. We stayed within the "safer" boundaries of what was going on at the pawnshop or at school. When we did talk about our situation it was never about how we felt but more about the logistics of our predicament. If I had it to do again, I would make us sit down and really discuss how we felt with each other. Instead, I tried to get each child into counseling.

THE NEW NORMAL

Life had shifted and I would have to adjust. My friend, Liz, called it the "new normal." The human spirit is remarkable in finding a way to adapt to a new situation. Like chameleons, we turn whatever color we need to be in order to survive. And with adjustment comes stress, anxiety, fear, and yes, loss. What a vicious cycle!

But eventually I did decide to take care of myself, just as I had taken care of Miller. After two months of driving to Charlotte every day and then to Cleveland every other weekend, I was exhausted by the efforts to keep my emotions under control. Sure, I cried, but in short spurts and with incriminations to myself about how I should be stronger for Miller and the kids. Finally, the floodgates opened and I was forced to deal with all the pent up feelings.

I gave myself permission to really feel the hurt, really experience the pain of my losses. Where was it written that I had to be strong and fearless and without emotion? I began to cry, sob, yell, scream, do whatever it took to really feel the sorrow and the pain. I'm not saying I was walking around crying all over everyone. I am saying that when I felt the grief bubble up while I was driving I would let the tears come. The front field, my driveway, my front stoop, all became places I could sob or scream fully and privately. I would let the tears well up and spill out during church services or in the shower. I just didn't hold back any more.

To some it may sound like a pity-party, like I was feeling sorry for myself. And although if you had said that to me at the time I would have asked you who had better reason to feel sorry for herself than I, it wasn't like that at all. It was more like seeing a lost and frightened child crying for his mother and reaching over and hugging the child until he catches hiss breath and feels better. Only I was the child and the comforter at the same time. According to one of my favorite authors, SARK, "If there is darkness, we have our flashlights. If there is terror, we have our God. If there is despair, fear, anxiety, or agony, we can become our own best parent and hold the child within us."

The second thing I did for myself was to fill my house and car with new music.

Since every song had some sad meaning now, I listened to Italian opera, Latino music, alto flute, guitar, piano and the classical music radio station instead of the classic rock station I usually listened to. I discovered Sarah Brightman and Andre Bocelli. I was lulled by *The Sounds of Wood and Steel* and *The Yearning*. I was enchanted with *Women of the Spirit*. The music was a balm to my soul, the background noise of my own personal movie.

Third, I went to see my doctor. Doctors are great in times like these. They cut right to the chase, your symptoms, and then give you a prescription. For almost an hour, I told my doctor what was going on in my life and listened to her advice about how I could take care of myself. I left her office with vitamins, brochures, and a prescription. I have never had to take much medication in my life, but I was not opposed to taking an anti-depressant to help me cope during this time.

My doctor explained how the medication she was prescribing worked and assured me it was not addictive.

As with a baby's tentative first steps, I was taking the first steps towards taking care of myself. I still felt like my head was under water, but I could feel it getting closer to the surface.

The Law of Gravity

It's harder to climb down than up. Gravity works against you not
with you.

Like the pull of the ego, it wants you to go faster into tomorrow,

so that today flashes by as the mountainside becomes a blur as you
drop.

But there might not be a tomorrow and yesterday you can no longer
see.

Climbing down means staying and paying attention to the present;
concentrating

on the moment—not too fast, not too slow.

You must grip the rocky edge and wait patiently for each tip of each
toe to find its hold.

And each movement brings you closer to the truth.

Why climb down? Because you have been to the top and it was flat
and icy

and you could see the distance of miles and feel the distance of
everything and everyone?

You want to come down and feel the earth securely underfoot; to feel
the soft moss

against your bare feet, to see the veins of the leaves and tap the
antennae of the snail.

Only God lives on high, yet, through us, He feels the pulse of
eternity.

4

"You gain strength, courage and confidence by every experience in which you really stop to look fear in the face. You are able to say to yourself, 'I lived through this horror. I can take the next thing that comes along.'"

—*Eleanor Roosevelt*

CLIMBING OVER FEAR AND DOUBT

What is your greatest fear? Is it your death? The death of someone you love? Being alone? Making a speech? I always thought mine was flying until I was enmeshed in the transplant drama. Now there were fears everywhere. There was the fear of driving to Cleveland alone. There was the fear of leaving my house unattended while I was away or, worse, left in the hands of my 18-year-old. There was the fear of getting sick and the fear of something happening to my children while I was away, fear they would be in a car wreck or put in jail. There was the fear of staying alone in a house in the middle of the woods at night. There was the fear of financial destitution. I was afraid of what I would face at the hospital and what I would face when I got home. I was afraid that people were stealing from the pawnshop. Fear permeated every pore of my body until I was paralyzed.

I began to see how irrational I was becoming and soon began to rely on a technique that I call "Worst-Case Scenario." Any time I would become afraid, I would say to myself, okay, what's the worst thing that could happen. For example, I'm driving to Cleveland and my car breaks down on the side of I-77 in between towns. What's the worst thing that could happen…I have a car phone, I have 24-hour roadside assistance with the Buick people, I have AAA. The car has locks; I would be safe until someone came to help me. The same with the children. If they ended up in the hospital or in jail I would get a good doctor or lawyer and deal with it. After all, wasn't I living a worst-case scenario now?

Finally, I had to let it go. Fear was literally wearing me out. I was exhausted by it and the only way to release it was to talk about it. I turned to the one person I had always been able to reveal my fears to, regardless of how rational or not they were—Miller. Since he could not leave the hospital, we spent our time together sitting around talking. He was allowed to leave the floor and so we would walk to other parts of the hospital and find great places to sit around. Since I was there on the weekends, there wasn't a lot of traffic from outpatients.

In the "P" building was a beautiful lobby for the Surgery Center, with deep, cushiony sofas and a sparkling fountain. On the way there from his room in the "G" building, there were little alcoves with loveseats and chairs, with a picture-window view of the busy street below. The skywalk to the "A" Building had a little nook by the elevator with leather wing chairs and looked out at the fountain in front of the hospital. We ate in the Founder's Dining Room and the cafeteria. We scanned the gift shop and the revolving art collection. We visited the "mini-museum" in The Children's Hospital where you can see old nurses' uniforms, doctors' instruments and technology from the past.

I would fill Miller in on what was going on at home. He would give me advice about the pawnshop and tell me the scoop on the other patients on his floor. Sometimes we would just sit and hold hands or curl up on his bed and hold each other. And I would tell him my fears. The good thing about Miller is his feistiness. He was a mischievous, scrawny kid in high school and I guess as the youngest of five he was used to defending himself. So it wasn't surprising that as I would tell him the things I was afraid of, he would bash each one. Like a baseball player hitting one home run after another, he would hit my fears one by one out of the park. It helped.

TRUST THE GUT

I don't think we give ourselves enough credit for what we can really physically and emotionally handle. We see things happen to other people and we think, I don't know what I'd do if that happened to me. Well, I'm here to tell you that you would deal with it one way or the other. The one sure thing is that no matter what happens, time does not stand still and you will be forced to move along too.

And we all have choices about how we will deal with our worst-case scenarios. Of course, in the middle of the worst case is usually not the best time to make decisions, so that's when you have to call on something outside yourself to guide you.

In my case, I have always had a strong intuitive sense, or gut feeling. I began to rely more and more on this gut feeling, which I believe is God within, to help me make the best decisions I was capable of making under the circumstances. I used God. Whenever fear crept in, I would pray that God would take care of whatever I was afraid of. I cried to Him, complained to Him, whined to Him. I begged Him to make my spinning-out-of-control world stop. Finally, one day I surrendered. I pulled out the white flag and gave up. In the grand scheme of things, this instance in my life was less than an eye blink to the universe. I had to trust that everything would work the way it was supposed to in its own time.

It's one thing to say you're going to "let go and let God;" it's another thing to actually do it. I think until I really, with my whole body and soul, believed that God was taking care of things, I couldn't let go. A friend once told me that if you choose to give control to someone else, it really means you are the one in control. In this case, I gained control of my life by giving control to God. It took practice, but in the end I was able to wake up and say, "Your will be done," and mean it. I knew that even if the worse case scenario happened, I would still go on and God would still be with me. In one of SARK's books, she quotes Patrick Overton, in his book *The Learning Tree*, and I think he puts it best: "When you walk to the edge of all the light and take that first step into the unknown, you must believe that one of two things will happen: there will be something solid for you to stand upon, or you will be taught how to fly." The trick here is that once you say it that's it, you can't take it back. It takes practice, but once you get the hang of it, fear seems to fade. The scary stuff doesn't go away; how you react to it does.

POWERING THROUGH

Another thing I would do is "power through" the fear. Like a bulldozer, when the fear would well up inside, I would just do whatever I was afraid of anyway. Eleanor Roosevelt once said, "Do what you think you cannot do." Most of the time it's not as scary as you think. The other side is a place of peace and confidence and freedom.

In moments of crisis I think we have our greatest moments of doubt. We're more vulnerable, especially to people who try to give us well-meaning advice. In my case, I had people telling me to move to Cleveland, to put Molly in private school (like I could afford this), to move out of the country and into town (like I could pack up a house and move during this time), to move back home, to rent an apartment in town and keep the house too, to visit Miller once a month instead of every other weekend, to take Molly with me to Cleveland and the hell with the attendance policy at her school, to leave her in Lenoir and be damned about feeling beholden to anyone, it went on and on. Every decision I was faced with had about nine different answers from nine different people.

I began to wonder: was I doing this right or not? I had no role model for this experience. Most of the other patients' wives either lived near enough to Cleveland so this wasn't an issue or were retired and moved to Cleveland and stayed in one of the hospital's Hospitality Homes. Despite what the social worker told me, I could not find one other wife doing the traveling I was doing.

I used to joke with Miller that it would have been better if the situation were reversed. I love to lie around and read all day. I would make an ideal transplant patient. He would be better at taking care of the business, home and disciplining our children. The irony of our situation was never lost on us. And maybe that was God's plan all along. It didn't make the doubt go away.

Finally, I asked Miller if our situations were reversed, how he would handle my end of it. He told me he would do the same thing I was doing. He told me I was being too hard on myself and that the best I could do was the best I could do. I drove the 500 miles back committed to letting myself off the hook.

In Terms of the Weather

In terms of the weather,
I'm not like the rain-washed,
crystalline-blue aftermath
of the storm.
Instead,
I'm like the time
in between storms,
when the air holds its breath
and a velvet gray shroud
suffocates the earth
and all earthly things.
With weighted arms, legs, torso,
I'm filled with the impending outcome.
The growing humidity begs my pores to weep.
Thunder rumbles between my ears.
I anticipate the downpour,
but really only want the sky,
in one magnificent crack,
to open
and allow the sun to sear
time away.

5

○ ○

"Being crabby is real and it's healing. It can help us get closer to what's wrong, or what hurts."

—SARK

GAINING PERMISSION TO BE NOT FINE

One of the most helpful things I did for myself was to visit the minister of a nearby Methodist church. She was a serious young woman who I had been referred to by a friend. She admitted to me that she wasn't a licensed counselor and the best she could offer was to listen and advise as one friend to another. Her sincerity and her objectivity were worth the visit. A few minutes into our conversation she asked me how I responded when someone asked me how I was doing. I said, "I say fine."

"But, don't you see," she said, "that when you say you're fine, you're denying how you really feel. Are you fine?" she asked.

"No," I said. "But I can't tell them I'm sad because I miss my husband and I'm afraid he's going to die. I can't tell them how my children are acting out and getting into trouble and that I just want to move to Cleveland and leave all this behind. People don't want to hear how you're really doing. They just want to know you're fine so they don't have to worry."

"But you are worth worrying about," she said. "By not telling them how you really are you're denying them the experience of helping you. And you're denying yourself their help," she said. "Every time you say you're fine, you send a conflicting message to your brain, which knows you're not fine. This conflict causes stress and anxiety and can make you depressed and resentful. You have to tell them how you really are."

"But how do I do that?" I asked.

"It's okay to say you're struggling. Tell them you're in a difficult situation right now and that you appreciate them asking," she said. "If they offer to help, let them."

I left her office feeling for the first time like I had an advocate for myself–me. I knew she was right. I had been so independent my whole life, never wanting to rely on anyone. Now I was going to have to learn how to lean on others for support. I was going to have to learn how to ask for help. As Natalie Goldberg says in her books on writing, you have to be kind to yourself.

So one day I decided to put this new philosophy to the test. It had been another horrible day. I was tired and didn't want to stop at the grocery store, but Mother Hubbard's dog had more to eat than we did. So I dragged myself behind a shopping cart. I was in the pet food aisle getting the Little Bites for the little dogs, the Fit and Trim for the big one, when around the corner came a woman from my church. Inwardly I sighed, no please don't make me have to talk to her, I thought. I put on the plastic smile as she asked me all about Miller. Then she did it; she asked the fateful question, "How are you doing?"

This is it, I thought. My chance to practice what the minister taught me. But what she had failed to tell me is that once the floodgates of truth are open they are impossible to close. I did start out with the nicey-nicey, "Oh it's a struggle without Miller" stuff. But once on a roll I couldn't stop myself. I began to go into every ugly detail about my life. I'm so tired all the time, I'm driving over 16 hours every other weekend, Molly was sick, I missed Miller and I was probably not going to be able to visit him this weekend because Molly was sick and that would mean I wouldn't see him for three weeks instead of two and there was no one to stay with her...it went on in what my eighth-grade science teacher used to call "diarrhea of the mouth."

I didn't hear the anger creeping into my voice either. But she did. Her eyes became big white baseballs and she began backing away from me, murmuring, "Oh dear, I'm so sorry." I was relentless. Each step she made backwards, I made towards her. I was a flamethrower. The freedom of truth was exhilarating. She suddenly turned on her heel and before she flew down the aisle and around the corner away from me she mumbled, "We're praying for Miller."

I stood alone in front of the dog food. The rushing in my ears disappeared and I could hear the quiet Eagles' tune playing through the grocery store. God, I'm a monster, I thought. She didn't know what hit her. I felt lousy.

I never did fully master how to respond to "How are you?" My mother had done her home training well. I just could not inflict my emotional pain on others because they were simply doing what they were trained to do. We ask how others are doing every day. Do we really want to know all the gory details? I think not. But maybe we shouldn't ask if we don't really care. You never know: one day the truth might come out and there we stand without our fireproof suits.

ASKING FOR HELP

It's a paradox. Never in my life have I needed help more, yet never in my life have I wanted to ask for help less. To ask for help means you're somehow not strong enough to handle everything. Admitting that could mean everything would then fall apart. If you walk around smiling, "handling" everything with seeming grace and confidence, then people assume you don't need any help. But if you walk around crying, downcast and depressed, people think you need help but you loose what little dignity you think you have in the process. Besides, in my case, how was I going to ask for help from people I barely knew? I wish I'd seen this quote by Anne Wilson Schaef during this time. She says, "Asking for help does not mean that we are weak or incompetent. It usually indicates an advanced level of honesty and intelligence." Well, I told you I was in denial and maybe my intelligence was impaired during this time.

The kind of help I needed was emotional. It became fairly easy to ask for help with the yard or the trash or the cars. What was impossible for me was to ask for emotional support. The kind that comes from having someone call and see how I was. Someone to come over and fill the lonely void that Miller left. Someone to hold me and tell me I was doing a good job holding everything together and that everything would be okay. I was like an animal caught in a trap. I was mobile enough to move around, yet unable to get anywhere. I kept waiting for someone to come release me.

But God always provides, even when we're down in a hole and we can't see our way out. In the midst of my loneliness came two particular friends, who called me on a regular basis to see how I was doing. Both have been friends since childhood. One I had remained close to. She was even the person Miller and I credit for getting us together. The other I hadn't seen in years, and her interest in my situation was wonderful. Her mother had cancer and I guess she knew what life was like for me. I will always appreciate her reaching out to me and I will try to keep her in my life from now on.

I am blessed with two brothers and a sister, with whom I'm close. They are better than just friends or relations. They know me and still love me. To say we've been through a lot together would severely underestimate our childhood and adulthood experiences. Each one gave love and support in ways that were unique and I will always be grateful.

Certainly one of my greatest sources of comfort came from being around the other heart transplant patients' wives. Like new mothers exchanging labor and delivery stories, we would eat in the cafeteria together and swap heart attack/heart failure stories. Our bonds tightened each time we heard someone had gotten a heart. Only we knew what that day would mean to us.

And we let each other off the hook for being crabby. We were all haggard. As hard as my life in Lenoir was, it was no picnic for them either. Living in other people's homes, staying in the hospital all day with husbands, who were weak or ill-tempered, coaxing sick spouses to eat, wishing there was something they could do to speed things up. I could see the weariness in their eyes. I could see the slight slump to their shoulders. We were gentle with each other, listening for long stretches to each other's doctor's reports, blood pressure readings, dietary changes.

Since they got to stay during the week, the other wives would fill me in on the latest news from the Transplant Special Care Unit. They knew all the nurses by name and tidbits about the nurses' lives outside the unit. They knew about the doctors, residents, and fellowship doctors. They knew who was going on the pump, the ventricular assist device, a pump implanted into a patient to assist the heart (usually put in the sickest patients). They knew how many hearts had been transplanted since their arrival and who hadn't made it.

They introduced me to the New York Deli and the Westside Market. They told me how to get to Wal-Mart and the mall. During the week, they visited Miller and could update me on his mental status. I envied the time they got to spend with their husbands, and mine, but at the same time it gave me a new appreciation for the "busyness" of my life at home. I felt like, for me, the waiting was going by a little quicker because of it.

Summer Night

Come quick!
There's a cool breath
coming through the window screen.
Let's go outside
and lie on white concrete.
And while the night sighs,
the moon will caress our cheeks
with damp kisses
and give us strength
to take the embrace
of another summer day.

6

○ ○

"While there's life, there's hope."

—Cicero

ATTITUDE IS EVERYTHING

I'd like to say a word about attitude here. You've probably heard it before, yet it's worth repeating. Attitude is everything. It's your only hope. As my sister says about maintaining a sense of humor during difficult times, "It's critical." It's the difference between making it and not. You can choose to have a fatalist attitude, convinced that the worst will happen, in which case you add fuel to the fire of your misery. Or you can take the optimistic approach and believe that things are going to work out. If you believe in cause and effect, if your intentions are that everything will be okay, then the effect is that it will. I believe that, in large part, we create our own experiences. If you think a certain way, your actions will reflect it, causing a result based on your initial thought. If I think Miller will get a heart and act as though he'll get a heart by saying "when" instead of "if" and by making plans for our future, then eventually he will get a heart. If I think positive, I'll act positive and soon positive things will happen. Sound flaky? Maybe, but for me it works.

When it came to attitude, Miller was the King. Instead of moping around, lying in bed all day in the hospital, he chose to spend his wait more constructively. The routine of hospital life can make time creep like a snail. Each day medications are given at the same time, food is delivered at the same time, and doctors visit at the same time. To create a diversion in his routine, Miller started walking all over the hospital in between the already scheduled activities. He walked in the basement, on the skywalks, through the lobbies. He walked in the mornings and in the evenings. By the time he got his heart, there were few hospital employees that didn't know him or hadn't seen him and his mobile I.V. pole walking the halls.

The patient menu was limited, and after months of eating the same things, Miller began saving his vegetables and low salt gravy to make his own version of beef stew. We affectionately referred to it as "prison stew." I would bring in vegetables and fruits, and Miller would make his own salads. I would make him different salad dressings and herb seasonings from the American Heart Association cookbook and he would use them on salads, chicken, and beans. Instead of whining about nothing to eat, he started creating his own dishes.

He was rarely idle. He sewed hearts out of red felt my mother sent him, stuffing them with cotton balls and giving them to other patients. He played his guitar and ordered rhythm kits (drums, triangles, kazoos, etc.) from one of our vendors to give to the children in the children's hospital.

The Cleveland Clinic has patients from around the world. People come from distant countries, as well as nearby cities and towns. For those without the money to afford a hotel stay, the large lobbies in the Clinic become dormitories at night. Some nights when I would leave, the lobby in the "F" building would not have an empty sofa or chair. Men, women and children of all ages would be sleeping or quietly talking, bags and suitcases at their feet, pillows at the ready. The hospital provides blankets for these people, but not everyone knows that. One night, on one of his walks, Miller saw an elderly couple without blankets. When you have walked the hospital as much as Miller, you learn where the linens are kept, so he got them a couple of blankets. From then on, he made it part of his nightly walking routine to check to see if anyone needed a blanket.

All this is important, in light of Miller's health. He may have been walking a few miles a day and cooking in his room, but don't let that fool you into thinking he was well enough to go home. It was the dobutamine that was keeping him active. One of his doctors once described dobutamine as being similar to "a whip beating an old horse to keep it going." Once we were eating in the cafeteria when Miller looked down and saw that his T-shirt was all wet. He pulled up his shirt and discovered a small leak in the tubing leading into his chest. He was leaking dobutamine. We hurriedly cleared the table and began the ten-minute walk back to his room. The drug is so powerful that by the time we got to his room, Miller could barely walk. He literally fell into bed. It was a quick reminder of the false sense of health we were living with.

I believe Miller's positive attitude helped him have a positive outcome. His walking, which made him stronger, resulted in a 3 hour surgery (whereas most take 4-6 hours). He helped others regain their positive attitudes by always appearing to be busy and lighthearted. His cooking and sewing became humorous, but they provided an effective way for him to stay sane during the wait, and when I joined him I became saner.

We tried to take the attitude that my visits were like mini vacations for both of us. I got away from the challenges of Lenoir; he got away from the mundane routine of the hospital. We played Canasta and Backgammon. We watched golf tournaments and old movies. We made salads and stew. And we walked. We walked!

Meditation

There is a millisecond
between heartbeats
when I am set free,
a short space
between breathing
out
and breathing
in,

Where the pressures of the heart
force an important decision—
to take the next breath
or not
beat again.

It's a silent spot of healing
that works its magic balm
of calm
and serenity
only if I sit quietly
and listen.

In this eternal space
I find
Eternity.
In this holy place
I find
Holiness.

An act of faith:
God lives between the beats.

7

"Never, never, never, never, never give up."

—*Winston Churchill*

NAVIGATING BY SIGHTS UNSEEN

My desk faces a field and a thick forest. Behind it lie larger foothills and the mountains. Many mornings I watch deer gently walk across the dew glistening field to disappear into the woods. Often they stop and graze right in front of my window. I wonder where they go and what they do when it rains or snows. Where do they find food in those conditions? How do they keep from getting sick in such cold? And then it hits me. God has given them instinct and camouflaged fur. He gives them shelter under dense forest canopies and bark on the trees to nibble when the leaves have turned brown and fallen. And I know, deep inside myself, that He protects me and provides for me too.

Faith is about never giving up. Despite all the turmoil, despite all the notions to the contrary, despite scary statistics, worst case scenarios and pessimists who proclaim doom and gloom, faith is a little voice inside of us that says, "That's not going to happen to you. Just don't give up."

My father wears an I.D. bracelet with "Never, never, never, never, never give up," engraved on it. This is a man who went to college at 16, had to drop out and support his mother at 18 and ended up owning his own company and becoming very successful by the time he was thirty. He has lost money in the stock market only to gain it all back and more. He has started several companies, one of which he, my brother and my brother's sons make a nice living from today. He's tenacious and he never gives up. He has never given up on my mother, a woman whose alcoholism has landed her in the hospital several times, in rehab and eventually the burn center at the University of North Carolina Medical Center in Chapel Hill. To me he is the epitome of faith. Faith in himself and faith in God.

Faith is the belief in sights unseen. It was early evening, not quite dark out, when I decided to take a walk across the field in front of our house. Winter cold had killed the tall grass and weeds it's usually thick with. As was becoming more and more usual, both Marson and Molly were spending the night with friends. I had been watching television and, when I left the house, I just left it on along with the lights in the living room, hallway, and my bedroom. I walked to the end of the field and turned to walk back. It was darker now and the stars glittered above me. As I approached the house, a strange sensation came over me. I saw the house, the yellow glow of the lights inside, the jittery images on the distant television screen. I stopped to stare. It looked like everyone was home. As I got closer, I "knew" that inside the house there was a father, probably sitting cross legged on the living room floor re-stringing his guitar, there was a mother in the kitchen cleaning up after dinner, there was a son, lolling in a blue leather recliner, watching his favorite sit-com, and there was a daughter, staring up at the ceiling of her bedroom, through her canopy bed, a phone cradled between her chin and shoulder. The outside scene of the house was the same, only the inside was different now. But if you were a total stranger, having come across the house after emerging from the woods, you would not know that inside the house was empty of people. You would assume there was human activity inside. I peeked in the picture window, into the living room. There were all the things, furniture, knick-knacks, photographs, I'd collected throughout the years. Everything was so the same, I expected Miller, Marson, or Molly to suddenly walk across the room and wave at me. Stepping back, I knew that would not happen. Would it be that way again, I asked myself? Yes, came the tiny voice, that lived somewhere over my diaphragm and which I'd come to rely on. This was the seed of my faith.

Faith is when you step off a ledge even though you can't see the net. It's my belief that there is a power greater than myself always at work in the universe. Is my destiny preordained? I don't think so. After all, I have free will. But if I believe that my higher power loves me and I listen to the inner voice of guidance and heed it, whether I intellectually think what I'm doing makes sense or not, then I believe I will always be okay and that I'm on the right path.

Oh, how sweet is surrender.

In Sickness and In Health

Before…
I couldn't see
the knuckles of your spine.
I couldn't hear
the echo in your breathing.
I didn't know
pharmacology.
Before…
I saw
only soft dimpled places.
I heard
only comforting rhythms.
I knew
nothing of pharmacology.

8

"Life is not promised to you. Nor is it promised that it will go the way you want it to, when you want it to."

—Rosalind Cash

THE PATH IS FULL OF FELLOW TRAVELERS

Whenever I started succumbing to self-pity, all I had to do was visit the patients on the 11th floor of the "G" Building, The Transplant Special Care Unit, in order to slap myself back into reality. The unit is lined on one side by windows, giving you a panoramic view of the Cleveland skyline. During the day you can see white sailboats on Lake Erie and the Goodyear Blimp hovering over the Browns' stadium on game days. At night it twinkles with a million stars and city lights. Directly below is the hospital's entrance. For the patients, many days and nights are spent sitting in front of the windows, chatting with family, reading, or just staring at the people below coming and going, in and out of the hospital.

Inevitably, I would arrive at the elevator in the Clinic lobby loaded down with tote bags and grocery bags full of food, gifts, and magazines for Miller and, even if I'd stopped at the last rest stop just outside the city, it never failed: I would always have to go to the bathroom. And just as sure, the elevator would be packed and stop at every floor. Finally, I would reach the 11th floor.

As I'd walk by the wall of windows, I'd come to the nurses' station on the right, and in front would be a wall-sized dry-erase board. Every patient in the unit is listed on this board. Despite my fatigue and the insistence of nature calling, I always stopped to examine the board. It didn't take me long to learn the board's code. All the patients listed with a CHF next to their names were other heart transplant patients. Sometimes there were as few as nine, other times there were as many as eighteen.

Miller's room was near the nurses' station. He was to be in five different rooms during his stay and have over twenty roommates. Each room has two beds, separated by a curtain. The bed by the window is usually for patients waiting for transplant. In the other bed there's usually a transient transplant recipient, back for tests, a biopsy, or a check-up. Sometimes it's a patient who can't be placed anywhere else because his floor is full.

Miller arrived on the 11th floor a week after his admittance. One of the first things they did was implant a Hickman catheter into his chest. This catheter goes into the heart. It allows a continuous drip of dobutamine, a life-sustaining drug, as well as easy access for drawing blood or adding other intravenous medications. The bag of dobutamine is hung from an I.V. pole on wheels. Because it is usually the only thing hung on the pole, patients tend to decorate the other arms on the pole. One man had Beanie Baby bats hanging on his pole. Others had American flags, sports pennants, or pictures of their family on theirs. Because Miller has been a cap collector his whole life, his pole became a mobile hat tree. Not too long after hanging caps on his tree, he began receiving caps from the visiting relatives of the other patients.

His first roommate was Jack, a handsome man in his late fifties. He had a trim white beard and clear blue eyes. A high stack of get well cards on the ledge by the window, plastic containers of food, family pictures, and crayon drawings posted on the wall made it obvious he'd been there for a while. We learned he'd been there three months. He and his wife, Elaine, became our teachers, showing us the ropes.

Jack taught Miller the political correctness of the floor. According to Jack, there were three important things to remember if you didn't want to look like a rookie: 1) never wear your pajamas on the floor, the regulars wore street clothes outside their rooms; 2) beg, borrow, or steal plastic trays for your I.V. pole so you can have easy access to candy, tissues, medicine, etc., whenever you need it; and the most important thing, 3) never, ever walk around with your urinal bottle (the little plastic jug that measured a patient's daily output of urine) hanging on your pole, yuck! Leave the bottle in the room, preferably the bathroom. Since Miller arrived at the hospital in a gown, naked underneath, I bought him some underwear, knit shorts and T-shirts in the hospital gift shop. Jack managed to scarf up three plastic trays for Miller's pole and as for the urinal bottle, well, Miller was on his own with that one.

While Miller was learning the ropes from Jack, I was finding out what I needed to know from Elaine. First, she took me on a tour of the floor, including showing me the kitchenette and the plastic utensils, coffee, creamer, and napkins I could use and where they were kept. She showed me where I could put food I brought from home and the importance of labeling what I brought. Down the hall was the big refrigerator where patients had an unlimited supply of Popsicles and ice cream. She showed me the computer room, a recreational area with puzzles, games, books, a T.V. and VCR with videos, and a computer for the patients to use.

Second, Elaine showed me how to get to the Westside Market. I believe a visit to Cleveland is not complete without a visit to the Westside Market. The outside is a feast for the eyes, ears, and taste buds. Vendors of every kind of fruit and vegetable imaginable entice you with big slices. There are fat Italian pears, dripping mangoes, pineapples, peaches, vine-ripe tomatoes, and long branches with succulent figs. Lettuce, beans and cucumbers spill over bins and crates. People push and shove and shout, bartering over peppers, onions, and cabbages. It's like the United Nations of produce stands.

When you step inside the Market, you feel as though you're lost in an Impressionist painting. Color and light play together in the intricate tile work, and mosaics that line the walls and barrel ceiling. Murals of fruits and vegetables, heavily carved posts and the enormity of the space blur your senses and create an emotional and physical hunger. I wanted to taste everything, from pirogues filled with bourbon-basted chicken to braided bread with dill and rosemary to frothy cream-filled pastry. Spices, teas, octopus, whole goat carcasses, jalapenos, cactus salad, cous cous, you name it, they have it. I had never been anywhere like it before and as Miller's fluid allowance became less and less through the coming months, I would go to the market time and again to get him the juiciest fruits I could find.

Elaine introduced me to some of the other wives. As time went by, although I spent most of my visits with Miller, I would rely on the other wives as consolation that I was not the only one going through this nightmare. Sometimes just seeing one of them pass by Miller's door would make me feel better. I was now a member of a select, silent sisterhood. Far from Lenoir, where no one understood what my life had turned into, to Cleveland where this group of women understood all too well.

As time went on, I would meet the other patients that would form Miller's group of friends. Besides Jack, there was Kelvin, another youngster like Miller, who had the notoriety of becoming the seventh patient in almost 800 transplant patients at The Cleveland Clinic who would receive a second heart transplant. He had been transplanted three years previously and then contracted a virus, which put him back in the waiting game a second time.

There was Jerry, a large man from Tennessee, waiting for four months. There was Ken, from Kansas and Tom from New York. Each one had his own story. But what I came to realize was that despite the different routes they'd taken to get here, they all had two things in common. They all needed a heart transplant or they would die. And they rooted for each other.

With the scary statistics of how few donors there actually are staring them in the face daily, you would think there would be competitiveness. But when someone got a heart, the group didn't sit around grumbling about whose turn it was. They cheered the person on. They cheered for anyone who got a heart, a liver, a kidney, or a lung. People getting transplants meant transplants did happen. And if it could happen for those other guys, it could happen for them too.

Every time a transplant happened there was cause for celebration. Miller and his other heart buddies would gather around the family of the recipient and share their tears of joy. They visited the intensive care unit, poles and all, to wish the person well and see first-hand the light at the end of the tunnel. They kept on top of that person's recovery and slapped him on the back as he was wheeled out to go home. They didn't slump away depressed that they weren't going home. Instead, they went back to the business of waiting, watching sports on TV, playing poker, chatting with relatives, walking the halls, going to C.H.I.R.P. (Cardiovascular Health Improvement and Rehabilitation Program), and taking their meds.

Their attitude was an inspiration for me. They understood that the waiting was out of their control and belly aching about it or begrudging another person's transplant wasn't going to get them any closer to theirs. If they could endure, then so could I.

SAVING GRACE

And then there was Grace. Grace was a woman about Miller's age with long blondish-brown hair, a wide innocent face, and an I.V. pole full of Beanie Babies. I don't know how long Grace had been waiting, but it must have been a long time because I could never find anyone who had been there before her. She had a very sick heart and so she had a ventricular assist device implanted in her body. This miraculous machine actually does the work of one of the chambers of the heart, allowing the patient to gain time as the heart weakens. You could always hear her coming because the whoosh-whoosh of the device's pump preceded her wherever she went. Most of the time she was accompanied by her mother, a short woman with waist-length white hair and a face etched with deep wrinkles. Both were inspirational. They were always upbeat, laughing and offering words of encouragement.

Grace didn't live on the floor with the others. She lived in the "P" Building, which had a floor for outpatient housing. This was where Miller would stay after his recovery period, since he would not be sick enough to stay on the unit but would be too unstable to be sent home.

The first time I heard Grace's name was from Elaine. It was one of my first visits and the scuttlebutt on the floor when I arrived was that there was a heart for someone. Who would get it? Elaine was desperately hoping it was Jack; silently, I hoped it was for Miller. Instead, we found out that Grace was the probable candidate. It was my first encounter with being passed over and I felt a twinge of resentment. As it turned out, Grace would not be getting the heart but would be implanted with the assist device instead. Suddenly I felt ashamed. Sure, I wanted Miller to get a heart. But wasn't the real point here that someone got a new heart that day? And more importantly, how did it feel to come so close, like Grace did, only to get a device that would just keep postponing things? And everyone on the floor knew the device wasn't the end-all or be-all for giving you more time. It had its own set of problems: infections could arise; your body could reject it just like it could reject a new organ. Suddenly I felt sorry for Grace. What a letdown for her and her family. Being put back in the waiting room when you'd been that close to leaving must be hard on your spirit, I thought.

But on one of my next visits, sitting in the computer room, I heard a whoosh-whoosh. It was Grace. Here I was face-to-face with someone I'd only heard about and the first person I'd ever met with a heart assist device. She saw Miller and her face lit up. He hugged her and introduced her to me. We began to talk and I soon learned that she was thankful to have the device and not angry she'd missed her chance at a heart. Her attitude was that the right heart for her would come along one day and she really wasn't worried about it. In the meantime, she would visit the other patients and their families and try to keep everyone laughing as much as possible. Miller laughed and told me that the last two people Grace had visited got heart transplants the next day. I secretly hoped that this visit would conjure up the fates to do the same for Miller.

Through the months, I looked forward to seeing Grace and talking to her. She had a quiet openness that drew you to her. With the innocence of a toddler and the wisdom of a crone, she was a paradox with her crooked smile and large watery eyes. She told me she knew Miller would get his heart and be okay. She told us to hang on and not give up. She always seemed more concerned with our states-of-mind than her own. She was quick to hug you or hold your hand.

That's why it seemed so unbelievable when she got an infection and went into intensive care. By this time, Miller had gotten his transplant and was in his last week at the P Building. I had come to take him home. As fate would have it, Jack was in the "P" Building too and Elaine was the one to bring us the news of Grace's admittance into intensive care. She said it didn't look good for Grace. We were stunned. If anyone should make it, Grace should. Didn't she hold up everyone else in the dark times?

We went up to the cardiac ICU. In the hall outside the unit stood her mother and some of her other relatives. I hugged her mother. The tears puddled in her wrinkled face. We went in to see Grace. She was pale yellow, her eyes shut. When she opened them they swam in blood. She smiled, the same crooked smile I'd grown to look forward to. Miller took her hand and told her she would be all right. I looked into her eyes and could tell she knew that she would not.

During Christmas, a cemetery just outside our town sets up a luminary display. It is a spectacular sight with a candle on every grave lighting the night with spirituality. I decided to drive through one night on my way home from the pawnshop. It was mystical as the long line of cars crawled through the dark graveyard, surrounded by hundreds of flickering candles. I couldn't help thinking about the person each candle represented, about their life and their family. As I got to the end and was pulling back out onto the highway, I looked back at this sea of sparkling lights and thought about all the healthy organs that had been buried because someone's next of kin couldn't face burying their loved one less than whole. How many lives could have been saved? According to our procurement agency, one person can enhance or save the lives of 50 others through organ and tissue donation. "You can't take 'em to glory," is how one of Miller's nurses so eloquently put it. I think God heartily approves of our ability to recycle life. If the families of potential donors would think of it as a way of co-creating with God instead of a "taking away" of what He's given us, I think they would be more willing to give this gift of life.

If only everyone was an organ donor, then Grace would have made it. Instead the infection finally took her. We were home by then and all we could do was cry and pray for her and her family. She was the most courageous person I've ever met. Her name fit her. I wish I could face the hardships and problems of my life with just one ounce of the grace she had.

The Birth of a Wave

Out in the ocean
Water swells in rhythm,
Gathering momentum,
And in one thrusting motion
Desperately reaches for heaven.
In a moment crystalline,
The wave rejoices, then succumbs
To the effort, overcome,
Breaking in roaring emotion.
Churning, spent, seeking solace,
It stretches frothy fingers
To the shore without success.
Grasping sand which disappears,
It retreats to Neptune's breast.

9

○ ○

"On earth, humans say, 'You owe me more,' in heaven, God and the angels say, 'Keep the change.'"

—*Barbara Mark and Trudy Griswold*
in ***The Angelspeake Book of Prayer and Healing***

ANGELS ALONG THE WAY

Miller and I arrived in Cleveland that first night at about 11:30 p.m. By the time he was settled in and I had seen he was safe in the ICU it was well after midnight. He had a bed, but I didn't. I stood in the unit wondering where I was going to sleep. Up since 5:30 the morning before, I was exhausted. The doctor told me there was a hotel attached to the hospital. Although it was one of the pricier chains, I decided it was the best place to go. I lugged my suitcase and pillow down an elevator, across two lobbies, up an elevator, through the long skywalk, and down another elevator until I stood at the hotel's front desk. I had one credit card with a $500 limit. Without realizing the daily rate, I told the cashier that I would be staying a week. I went to my room and fell into bed. The phone rang. It was the front desk telling me my credit card wouldn't approve the amount I needed. I felt the panic rise in my throat. "I don't have another credit card," I explained. I hear only silence from the other end. "What if I go to the ATM machine and get out enough money for tonight, will that help?" I asked.

A soft voice answered, "Don't worry about it, Mrs. Nance. You get a good night's sleep and we'll figure something out tomorrow." An angel had spoken.

As it turned out, my brother, Andrew, faxed his credit card information to the hotel the next day for me. And so another angel stepped in.

After realizing the expense of a hotel was way beyond our budget and the insurance company was not going to reimburse my travel expenses, I prayed that I would figure something out. The hospital offered Hospitality Homes, where patient family members could stay with someone who offered a room in their home for $15-$20 a night. These homes were in neighborhoods around Cleveland and most of the wives of the other patients stayed in them. I had a call in to the woman in charge of this type of housing when one day I received a phone call from Jay, an old friend I hadn't seen in years. He said he had heard of Miller's situation and that he had a brother that lived in a small town about thirty minutes from Cleveland. He told me he had already called his brother to see if I could stay with him and his brother had said yes. I was stunned. I called his brother and was invited to stay with him and his wife whenever I visited Miller. He laughed and said they had my room ready for me whenever I needed it.

Angels are hidden in the most amazing places. For me they were Jeff and Laura Williams of Hudson, Ohio. They opened their arms wide and took me in. There was a beautiful room with a soft, warm bed. Laura, an incredible cook, always had delicious, hearty meals waiting for me when I woke up and when I came home from the hospital, no matter how late I got in. Jeff filled my life with the laughter and stories and the fellowship of friendship. They and their two delightful children, Bobbie and Angela, became my every-other-weekend family. They took care of me and I basked in their love. It healed the rough spots of my life and made my trips to Cleveland something I looked forward to and hated to leave.

The most amazing thing is that to them it was no big deal. You would have thought they had complete strangers staying in their guest room all the time. Everything was business as usual, whether I was there or not. There were hockey practices and football practices, hockey games and football games, there were riding lessons and gymnastics, and there were dinner dates and babysitters. I felt like another member of the family, coming and going as I pleased, with a hot meal and a soft bed ready for me when I needed it. Their no-strings-attached generosity allowed me to move freely without the burden of being obliged. I cannot begin now or ever to thank them enough for their overwhelming kindness.

Angels never hesitate to help. That fateful day in Charlotte, when we had just received the bad news and Miller was going through the rigmarole of being admitted, my job was to find someone to come help at the pawnshop so I could stay with Miller. Numb and soggy from crying, I called my husband's cousin Lewis, our business partner. With a throat thick with emotion, I explained to him the situation and asked if he could come to Lenoir. Without hesitation he said he would be there in four hours. That's how long it takes to get to Lenoir from Fayetteville.

The same thing happened when I called my younger brother, Andrew. I needed someone to watch over the house, my children, and my three dogs while I was in Cleveland. Marson was scheduled to start college in a week and I would also need help moving him to his dorm. An independent sales rep, Andrew was the one person I knew who had the flexibility to leave his home, wife, and children to come help me. He was our family "rescuer," the kind of guy who will drop everything to help you move. He came the next day and stayed until we got Marson all moved in. I called Lewis and Andrew my Knights-in-Shining-Armor but I think angel describes them better.

When we found out we were going to The Cleveland Clinic, I had twenty minutes to get my stuff from across the street at the Charlotte Hospitality House and get back before the trauma team took Miller to the airport. I ran through the hospital and across the parking lot to the Hospitality House. I gathered up my bags and flew down the stairs to the office to check out. That's when it occurred to me I would have to leave my car. Now, the car at the time was less than three months old. How was I going to leave my brand new car in Charlotte? I called Penelope, one of my clients, and asked her if she would be willing to pick up my car and park it at her house. Without hesitation she told me she would take care of it. Not only did she take care of my care, she picked me up from the airport when I returned nine days later. I'm telling you, angels are everywhere.

Angels give support any way they can. My older brother, Herb, spent a day with Miller and me in the ICU in Charlotte. He brought his laptop computer and entertained us with a digital photo album of his family's vacation at the beach. He ate lunch with me in the cafeteria and it was wonderful having him there. When he heard I was driving back and forth to Cleveland, he loaned me his gas card, which saved me hundreds of dollars.

My sister, Cristi, was always available to me by phone. No matter if I called her at work or at home, she always had time to listen. She came to visit me in Lenoir while Miller was in Caldwell Memorial as well as when he was in Cleveland. And the week I spent in Richmond helping her with wedding plans was as much respite for me as anything else. She even braved a snowstorm to be with me when Miller had the transplant, only to have to turn back, since roads were closed and visibility was nil.

My mother called every week and sent Miller a "care" package of goodies every week he was in Cleveland. My grandmothers were there with emotional and financial support, as were Miller's uncle and brothers and sisters. His oldest sister,

Martha, came twice to Lenoir to stay with Molly. The list of things our family did for us goes on and on. The fact that we are scattered over three states didn't matter. I learned over and over again that angels live in your own family too.

I would be remiss if I didn't take this opportunity to mention all the angels on every floor and at every station and in every room of every hospital. These doctors, nurses, patient care technicians, social workers, therapists, laboratory assistants, and staff dedicate their lives to caring for others. To me there is a special aura about hospitals and each person who works in one radiates with it. It was these angels who gave us time and again the hope and encouragement and information we needed to make it through each day. I will be eternally grateful to them all.

A VISIT FROM MY ANGEL

It was the weekend before Thanksgiving. I knew I would not be spending Thanksgiving with Miller. We had agreed I should spend it with my parents so I could be home with Molly until her Christmas break. We would all come back for a long weekend at Christmas.

For some reason I decided to pay a visit to St. Paul's Episcopal Church that Saturday morning before going to the hospital. Rev. Nick White and Deacon Kirby Colwell had consistently visited Miller every week since he'd been hospitalized. It meant a lot to Miller, and me, for Miller to have clergy support in a city where Miller knew no one, so I decided to thank them in person.

St. Paul's is an historic church in the Cleveland Heights section of Cleveland. It is only a few miles from The Cleveland Clinic. While at the church, I met a young, black woman in the ladies' room. It seemed she was a member of the choir from St. Augustine's College in Raleigh, North Carolina, which would be performing the next day. I was amazed at how much comfort I got hearing her southeastern North Carolina accent, and she told me she would have the choir pray for Miller. I told her I would come back to hear them sing. The next morning I saw her again in the vestibule of the church. She recognized me and waved.

There was a tall, elderly woman standing next to the guest book, where I signed in. When she saw my North Carolina address, she politely asked if I were here visiting relatives. I explained about Miller and her face lit up. She introduced herself and told me her son was an Episcopal minister at another church in Cleveland and he had gone to visit Miller. Miller's name was on their prayer list as well. She squeezed my hand and told me that if I ever needed a place to stay while in Cleveland, I could stay with her.

I moved into the sanctuary, not sure where to sit in this massive space. The ceiling was high, accommodating a beautiful pipe organ. There were ornate columns and row on row of polished pews. There was a large gold cross suspended over the altar. It was breathtaking and by far the largest Episcopal church I had ever been in. I took a seat at the end of a pew near the front and behind one of the columns.

The woman I'd met at the guest book sat down in the pew in front of me. She turned around and invited me to sit with her and her friends so I would be able to see better. I moved up to her row.

The St. Paul's choir sits behind an ornate wooden screen and as they began to sing there was an ethereal quality to my surroundings as the service began. The acolytes and St. Augustine's choir processed in ahead of the deacons and ministers of the church. The comfort of knowing I was reciting the same words from the same prayer book and at the same time as the folks back home was tremendous. I felt part of a huge family. I was immediately glad I had come.

I have a habit of closing my eyes when listening to the choir and today was no different. I closed my eyes as the St. Augustine's College choir began a rich, full-bodied Negro spiritual. My heart vibrated with the longing of the song. I felt as though they were singing about my life. The music first surrounded me and then ran through me. I let myself be carried away, almost in a trance, as I began to feel a wonderful warmth surround my body. It felt as though someone was standing behind me, wrapping such loving arms around me I wanted to stay there forever. I had never had such a feeling before. It was as if the nervous tension of a tightly strung harp string was suddenly loosened, to dangle limp and relaxed. For the first time in months, I felt the knots loosen in my stomach and the air flow easily in and out of my lungs. I felt worry-free. It was wonderful.

I cracked an eye open for a second and saw soft white feathers encircling the front of my dress. I could see the arm-length white quills in the center of wide pearlescent feathers. Their tips were the color of pristine snow, sparkling with sun. I closed my eye tight again.

When I opened both eyes, I saw the "guest-book" woman beside me. She was intently watching the choir. Nothing in the church had changed. Except me. The anxiety I had been lugging around like a giant boulder between my shoulders was gone. Instead, I felt reassurance and a deep down knowing that everything was going to be okay. I breathed easier and I knew in that moment I had been embraced by an angel.

ANGELS ARE EVERYWHERE

Throughout my journey, one thing became more and more evident. The world is full of angels. Not just the celestial ones that appear in magical moments like my encounter at St. Paul's. But everyday angels who lend support, find just the right word, or offer a hand to hold and help move us forward while we plod along. They're our landladies and bosses. They're at gas stations and fast food restaurants. They're at hospitals and Wal-Marts. They're in parking garages and churches. They're strangers who say just the right things at just the right moment, filling you with comfort and hope. They're the "answerers" of our prayers. All you have to do is listen to their kind words, see the softness in their eyes and the friendliness of their smiles to know they are all around us, all the time.

The Hike

We step
into the dark canopy
of the forest,
beginning our hike
at its beginning:
the path is narrow—
one at a time
can it
accommodate;
rhododendrons bow
at our entry;
beaver-carved trees
stand as sculptures
of a civilization left humanless.
Like the original couple,
we alone walk
upright in the woods.
At first,
we hear only the sound
of ourselves.
Heartbeats and breathing.
Sole against rock and root.
The comfort of a creek bed
brings respite; we rest by its side.
Familiarity with the forest
heightens our hearing.
Slowly, we notice
nature harmonizing—
the rhythmic rustle
of a hidden dance in the leaves
by bird or squirrel;

the soft clapping
of water lapping
stones;
the hawk's seductive song;
then, silence as strong as any symphony.
We are sojourners—
discovering a prehistoric world.
Sticking our fingers into the pitcher plant,
tasting the sweetness of the honeysuckle,
smelling the earth recycling and renewing herself.
We slow down
with the thought
of departure.
The path leads
the way out.
We step out
of the dark canopy
of the forest,
ending our hike
at its ending.

10

"Nature is God's great revelation of himself, his richness, his complexity, his intelligence, his beauty, his mystery, his great power and glory."

—*Luci Shaw*

THERE'S NURTURE IN NATURE

I have always loved being outside. Camping, horseback riding, hiking, playing golf, or swinging in a hammock reading a good book, I would always rather be out than in. So it's no surprise that being outside became my safe place. Miller was hospitalized in July. The sights and smells of summer were every-where…emerald and chartreuse leaves dappling a cerulean sky, white, puffy clouds, the smell of new mown grass all wet and clingy, the earthiness of the for-est recycling itself, chickadees, goldfinch, cardinals, and hummingbirds harmo-nizing, singing because it was summer and there was plenty to eat, the wind whispering and ruffling the leaves, the brilliance of zinnias in fuchsia, orange and yellow sunbursts, the buzzing bees tiptoeing on clover pom-poms. I would sit on my patio each morning, drinking coffee and taking deep breaths of nature. God is nearer to me there than anywhere. The silence was soothing too, when nature took a breath and for a split second there was only the sound of the air.

As I began to travel to Ohio and back I began to notice the subtle changes of the seasons. While we were wrapped in green in North Carolina and Virginia, West Virginia was beginning to show signs of crimson and gold and Ohio was like a bejeweled dowager, glistening in her finery. As the colors marched south-ward, the north became a wasteland of barren trees, showing hidden rocks and crevices. By the time the south had shed its vibrant robes, the north was covered in a white flannel gown of snow. There was something magical about starting out in one color and ending in another, like Dorothy and the Wizard of Oz, black and white to Technicolor and then back again. I felt as though I was a gypsy who could foretell the future, who could see into another realm. There was a strange sense of comfort in knowing that no matter what was going on in my life, life itself would go on. The leaves would turn colors, then turn brown and fall, then the snow would come and soon be gone only to be replaced with new growth and the cycle would continue as it had from the beginning of time. I was just another part of the cycle.

There is also great comfort in stargazing. I am lucky to live in a place where there are no street lights or lights from buildings and cars. At night, out in the country, the only light comes from the moon and the stars. On clear nights, the stars surround you and it's easy to pick out the Big Dipper and the Little Dipper, which are about the extent of my knowledge of astronomy. But their masses are magical. To think they are billions of miles away and by the time a single thing would get to one star my life would be long over is awesome. It trivializes all my problems down to the size of an atom.

The phases of the moon are always the same. The moon is turning, we are turning and the light of the sun never leaves us. I especially love a full moon where I live because it shines through the shutters of my bedroom window and the slats make a pattern on the carpet identical to the pattern the streetlight used to make through my childhood bedroom window. The comfort in that familiarity is indescribable.

Nature survives year after year. Bluebirds build nests, deer graze on the azaleas, and the old magnolia tree broken in half by a storm sprouts new growth. Nature is hard on its inhabitants, yet they still manage to make it. They evolve and adjust, without complaint or hassle. Animals and plants just do what they have to do to stay alive. As I walked through the rain in the woods in front of my house or drove past black squirrels hopping through yards in Ohio, I knew that I too would survive the storm I was in.

I Am Sleep

I am sleep.
Coaxing, in comforting
whispered tones,
my invitation
to dark, warm safety.

I am sleep.
The arbiter of time,
patting excited minds
into simultaneous hibernation.

I am sleep.
The great escape,
offering truths
in a cinematic
soothing balm.

I am sleep.
Taking the burden
off your back
and offering you
a robe of respite.

I am sleep.
Kissing lids closed,
rubbing the ridges
off foreheads and faces,
slowing the rhythms of reality,
a cradle for the weary.

11

"Life is a series of relapses and recoveries."

—*George Ade*

CREATING CREATURE COMFORTS

My daughter once wrote a sermon for Youth Sunday at our church entitled "Angels In Fur Coats." In it she suggested that dogs and cats were angels in disguise. I think she may have been right. I have always lived with a dog, sometimes several, and sometimes with cats. But dogs have been a constant throughout my life. I have three dogs now, two rat terriers and a Labrador retriever. As dog lovers will tell you, nothing beats coming home from a hard day and being greeted by a dog. You can leave your house to take out the trash and when you return your dog will greet you like you've been gone for weeks.

Working at home, I have developed a very close relationship with my dogs. My dogs sleep all around me when I write. I type to the synchronization of their snores and the rhythms of their breathing. Without a word they understand everything about me and sympathize with all my problems. Although, sometimes I feel like my purpose on earth is to let them in and out of the house. I saw a T-shirt the other day that showed a page off a legal pad with the words: "Agenda: let dog in, let dog out, let dog in, let dog out."

Their presence softened the edges of loneliness. While Miller was away, the two smaller dogs, Mike and Minnie, had free rein of our bed, the most desirable place to sleep in the house if you're a dog. At night, I would reach out and touch their warm fur and rest my hand on their rising and falling backs. It was nice to have someone to sleep with.

COMFORT FOOD

Staying with Laura Williams in Hudson, Ohio, was like living in a restaurant. She brought a whole new meaning to the joy of cooking. Despite having only a husband and two small children to feed, she cooked on a larger scale and with a gusto I've never seen before. She didn't cook a casserole dish of lasagna; she made a tray of it. Her soups came in 16-quart stock pots. Her apple pie was like a pyramid on a ceramic pie dish. Her cheese came in restaurant-size rounds. Everything was fresh, nothing was wasted, and everything was delicious. She inspired me to make my own bread and homemade soups, and to plant an herb garden. Thanks to Laura, I now put honey on my buttered toast, cook more kielbasa, and make soup from scratch. The term "comfort food" took on a whole new meaning for me. Kneading bread became my therapy, and slicing London broil very thin for thick sandwiches to take on the road became a religious experience. I began to eat healthier than I ever had.

But the biggest payoff came in the preparation. In order to cook starting from scratch and using everything fresh, you have to concentrate, something that I'd found hard to do. But reading the recipe and following each step was a manageable amount of concentrating. I found that true bliss is in concentration. I could lose myself in the chopping and measuring and sautéing. I could escape into the batter and the dough and the stock. When you have all the ingredients and plenty of time, nowhere can tranquility be found better than in cooking.

AROMATHERAPY

Smells get to me. A whiff of perfume in a department store can either ruin or enhance the rest of my shopping experience. The lingering scent of someone's perfume as she walks by my table in a restaurant can conjure up memories of my mother. Jergen's lotion will forever remind me of my grandmother and take me back to her black-and-white tiled bathroom, where the Jergen's bottle always sat next to the sink. I wake to the smell of coffee and go to sleep to the smell of Gain, the detergent I wash my sheets in. I can smell rain coming. While Miller was in the hospital I discovered that smells could have a calming influence in my life.

One afternoon I visited the spa next to my doctor's office and went on a "sensory journey." The aromatherapy consultant had me sit in a comfy chair, close my eyes and listen to soft music. Then she proceeded to wave small vials of essential oils under my nose as I told her whether I liked each smell or not. Every so often she would wave a vial of coffee under my nose to clear away or neutralize the other smells. Finally, we narrowed my choices to one. It's a rose-based smell and she told me it was associated with fire and warmth. When I told her what was going on in my life, she said she wasn't surprised this smell appealed to me. She said that smells help balance the chemistry in your body, and the aroma you choose is what your body is craving at the time to put it back in balance. The aroma I had chosen would help me fill the need for comfort in my home and surroundings. I was craving the warmth of my family. Using my chosen aroma, the consultant mixed me a bottle of hand lotion and I purchased the essential oil so I could make my own aromatherapy products. Using *"The Natural Beauty & Bath Book,"* I made my own bath oil, body oil, massage oil, body powder, bath salts, and soap. As with the cooking, I could get lost in the recipes.

The hunt for the ingredients became a quest. After all, it's hard to find Dead Sea salts in Lenoir. Locating French clay and aloe vera gel, tea tree extract and sweet almond oil, gave me a new purpose in life. Next it was finding bottles and containers for my concoctions that filled my mind. The Pompeian olive oil bottle held my witch hazel astringent and large decanters were filled with rosewater and glycerin. A jar for sprinkling cheese held my body powder, while mason jars were perfect for bath salts. Soon I was mixing and sifting and funneling all kinds of beauty products in my kitchen. It was messy but smelled like heaven.

POETIC YEARNINGS

Since concentrating was a major issue during that time, I found it almost impossible to read novels, so I turned to poetry. With poetry, a door opened and out came all my feelings and emotions in the words of other people. In Emily Dickinson I found my desperateness and the fear that I wouldn't be there for Miller if he needed me:

> "I should not leave my friend,
> Because—because if he should die
> While I was gone, and I—too late—
> Should reach the heart that wanted me;
> If I should disappoint the eyes
> That hunted, hunted so, to see,
> And could not bear to shut until

They "noticed" me—they noticed me;
If I should stab the patient faith
So sure I'd come—so sure I'd come.
It listening, listening, went to sleep
Telling my tardy name,—
My heart would wish it broke before,
Since breaking then, since breaking then,
Were useless as next morning's sun,
Where midnight frosts had lain!

Edna St. Vincent Millay put words to how it felt to live my life:

When I too long have looked upon your face,
Wherein for me a brightness unobscured
Save by the mists of brightness has its place,
And terrible beauty not to be endured,
I turn away reluctant from the light,
And stand irresolute, a mind undone,
A silly, dazzled thing deprived of sight
From having looked too long upon the sun.
Then is my daily life a narrow room
In which a little while, uncertainly,
Surrounded by impenetrable gloom,
Among familiar things grown strange to me
Making my way, I pause, and feel, and hark,
Till I become accustomed to the dark.

Elizabeth Bishop, Luci Shaw, Walt Whitman, Dylan Thomas, Robert Frost, Rainer Marie Rilke, I sought comfort in their words and in their thoughts. And I was never disappointed in what I found. It spurred me on to write my own poetry. I would bring my notebook to the cafeteria in the hospital and write while eating dinner. I would sit in front of the fire in my home office on my "at home" weekends and write. I would sit at Laura's kitchen table, early in the morning before the others got up, writing. It was therapeutic and easier for me than keeping a journal. The poems throughout this book were written during this time.

SLEEP: THE GREAT HEALER

A final word on creature comforts. One of the most important things you can do for yourself any time is get plenty of sleep. I've always been a big nap taker. I was the little girl who told her mother when it was naptime instead of the other way around. When I was little, if I was tired I'd take a nap and it didn't matter where I was. I can remember taking naps on the cool linoleum kitchen floor. As an adult, I would put my children in my bed in the afternoon so we could all take a nap. To this day, I take a nap almost every day around 2:00 p.m. (Why do you think I work for myself?)

When you're in a stressful time in your life, a nap is the only way to recharge a failing battery. It's an escape route, even if for only a few minutes. Once again SARK says it best in her poster called "*Change Your Life Without Getting Out Of Bed,*" "We need tender places in which to repair our souls and put special glue on the broken places. We replenish and repair during naps." It's true; just ask any kindergarten teacher.

Lessons In Survival

Get plenty of sleep.
Take your vitamins.
Check your energy fields.
Take it one day at a time.
Try Gavescon.

Exercise.
Eat your veggies.
Attend a healing service.
Pray without ceasing.
Ride a moped.

Give it to God.
Ask for help.
Change doctors.
Ask questions.
Write it all down.

Be positive.
Take enzymes.
Examine the alternative.
Give up caffeine.
Get an adjustment.

Stay in the present.
Walk on a treadmill.
Do what it takes.
Get through
Another day.

12

"There are no meaningless experiences."

—*Susan L. Taylor*

ONE JOURNEY ENDS WHILE ANOTHER BEGINS

It was the week of Christmas. Marson, Molly and I, along with Miller's brother, Mark, stayed in a beautiful home in Cleveland Heights loaned to us by a family who attend St. Paul's. We had the house from December 23rd until January 5th, if we needed it that long. We spent Christmas day opening presents in Miller's bed, drinking sparkling cider and playing Canasta. As a special treat, we ordered Chinese food and had it delivered to the hospital. We laughed and enjoyed meeting the visiting relatives of the other patients. It had been weeks since the last heart transplant.

I was supposed to leave two days later, but I saw something in Miller's eyes that told me to stay. His light-hearted, joking manner was beginning to disappear under the strain of waiting. His energy was running out. We arranged for a rental car and Mark took the kids home. A few days later, in an attempt to lift his spirits, I suggested we start loading my car with some of the things Miller had accumulated after four and half months in the hospital, start getting ready for his transplant. We started boxing and bagging up the stuffed animals, Carolina Panther pennants, candy, fruit, and stacks of get well cards he had received. On one of my return trips from the car, I saw the Charge Nurse waving me to the nurse's station. "We got a call for Miller," she said, her eyes bright and watery.

I didn't understand. I said, "What do you mean, a call?"

"There's a heart for Miller," she said. My own heart stood still.

"Have you told him yet?" I asked.

"No, let's go tell him together," she said.

We walked into Miller's room. It was about 5:00 p.m. and he was alone; his roommate had been discharged that morning. He was sitting on the side of the bed, putting T-shirts into a box. The nurse held my arm and I managed to say, through eyes thick with tears and a throat tight with emotion, "Miller, they have a heart for you."

"No! Are you sure?" he said in disbelief. The tears started to stream down his face, into his smile. And we all began to hug and laugh until others started coming in the room.

"We'll take you to ICU and get you ready, but you have to remember there's still a chance it may not happen," the nurse explained. "The heart may be badly bruised or the family may change their mind." It didn't matter; we were ecstatic.

The first thing on our mind was how to get the kids back to Cleveland. Mark had left them in Lenoir and proceeded on to West Virginia to go skiing. The other closest relative we could think of who would go to Lenoir and pick up Molly and Marson was Miller's older sister, Martha, who lived in Atlanta. But, when we called, her daughter, Meg, told us she was in California visiting friends.

"I'll do it!" Meg excitedly told us. "I'll be happy to go to Lenoir and bring them to Cleveland." We were elated.

"All I remember is getting in the car and going!" said Marson, when we talked later about what happened. "I was at the house, it was after work and I just remember getting a call and then Meg came and spent the night and the next day I drove about eighty miles an hour to Cleveland. Meg let me drive because I knew the way. I had butterflies in my stomach pretty bad!"

Molly was at work that night. She was the hostess in restaurant at a local golf center. "When Marson came in and told me Dad got a heart, I went in the kitchen and screamed real loud! I felt overwhelmed, full of joy and happiness, and as if a heavy burden was off my shoulders. The release of waiting was overwhelming. I just started crying."

Since there was still the chance the new heart could be too bruised to use or other complications that would send Miller back to the unit without a new heart, we decided to wait and call other family and friends until Miller was in surgery. We had seen Jack and Elaine go to surgery twice, only to return to the unit because the hearts weren't useable for whatever reason. We didn't want to get the rest of the family excited before we were sure this wasn't a "dry run."

At 5:30 p.m., December 29, 1999, Miller went into the ICU to begin the process of getting ready. He was unhooked from his I.V. pole, the first time the two had been separated in five months. Instead of dobutamine, he would now receive his anti-rejection medications. Instead of one monitor over his bed, he was now hooked to six. While we waited we prayed together, asking God to be with Miller and his doctors during the surgery and also that He be with the family of Miller's donor. Their sorrow was uppermost in our minds as we thanked God and them for giving Miller such a precious gift.

At 9:15 p.m., the transplant was declared "a go." But despite being ready, Miller again had to wait a little longer while they prepped a patient who had just been brought into the ICU. Her name was Debbie and she would receive the lungs from the same donor who would give Miller a heart. Both Miller and Debbie were wheeled out around 10:00 p.m. I walked beside Miller's gurney as far as the operating room door. With one last kiss, our tears commingling on each other's faces, we said good-bye. I felt peaceful and joyous at the same time. I heaved a huge sigh as the operating room doors closed.

During the operation I was pumped with adrenaline. I called everyone we knew. In my excitement I called some twice. The reaction was the same from everyone, elation, happiness, thankful. Despite the heavy snowfall outside, Miller's brother, Max and his wife, Judy, along with Miller's other sister, Mary Lou and her husband and kids, Kurt, Jon, and Mackenzie, planned to make the trip from their homes in Fayetteville and Fredericksburg, Virginia, to see Miller. My sister would try to come from Richmond, although the system that had brought the snow to Cleveland was headed in her direction.

After I was sure everyone we knew had been called, I spent two and half-hours cleaning Miller's room. He had accumulated so much stuff over the past months, it took me two hours just to go through it all, throw stuff away and pack up boxes. When they told me he had too much stuff to put in the hospital storage room, I had to hunt down one of the Clinic's policemen to ask permission to double park my car in front of the hospital. With everything piled in a wheel-chair, it took me three trips to get everything into my car. When it was packed, the trunk was full and I couldn't see out the back window. I had the energy of three women and I barely noticed it was snowing!

It's funny but I was never once concerned that Miller wouldn't make it through the surgery. The doctors and told us in the very beginning that it was the wait that most patients didn't survive, not the surgery. In fact, only about five percent of patients died during surgery. This is why the cardiac rehabilitation program and the walking are so important. If a person can keep the rest of their body in fairly good shape before the surgery, the chances of surviving it are improved. And Miller had certainly done that! I just knew that if he could make it to the surgery, he would make it through that as well.

By the time I got back to the family waiting room outside the ICU, there was a note telling me the surgeon had stopped by and said Miller's surgery was over and that he had come through just fine. Miller's surgery had taken only three hours—half the amount of time it usually took! By 1:20 a.m., December 30th, he was being sewed up, the recipient of a new, strong heart.

I was disappointed at having missed seeing the surgeon and furious at Miller for having so much stuff. I was sweating and huffing and puffing. But suddenly it hit me—it's over. The wait was over! I called into the ICU and was told I could come back for just a minute.

The ICU was hushed. Only the tiny lights of monitors and the lamp at the nurses' station illuminated the area. As I approached the curtained cubicle where Miller was sleeping, I stopped to stare at the chest x-rays beside his nurse's desk. The black and white image glowed. I could see the heart, Miller's new heart, and a tiny row of what looked like twist ties going up the center of the picture. The reality pounded in my brain. They had taken a saw and opened Miller's chest and removed his weak, sick heart and replaced it with the healthy one. Then they had twist-tied his breastbone back together and sewed him up. It was a miracle!

I smiled at the nurse, who was busy recording data on a large flow sheet. I stepped up to Miller's bedside and stroked his forehead with my fingertips. He had a tube taped to his mouth and his tongue hung limp over his bottom lip. I watched him sleep. I watched his chest go up and down. He had survived. We had survived. I was exhausted. I kissed his forehead and left to go enjoy the deepest, most satisfying sleep I'd had in years.

Miller's brother, Max, sister-in-law, Judy, and sister, Mary Lou, arrived the next day along with Meg and our children. (Yes, everyone's name in his family starts with an "M".) This was to be the best New Year's Eve we'd ever had. The new millennium heralded a new life for us in more than average significance. Since we could only visit Miller in the ICU until 10:00 p.m., I went to the grocery store and bought cheese, crackers, and a bottle of sparkling cider for an impromptu party. We all gathered at the house in Cleveland Heights and toasted Miller, his donor, his doctors and nurses, and the New Year.

Everyone except Meg and the kids left before midnight. While the kids watched on the television upstairs the ball in Times Square drop, Meg and I perched on stools watching the television in the kitchen. When it hit the ground, we cheered and Meg and I started crying. Suddenly, we heard bells and fire works outside. We went to the back porch and stood in the chilly night listening. The church bells from St. Paul's rung out loud and clear. A feeling of what I can only describe as grace washed over me. A miracle had taken place in my life and now it was as though the whole world felt miraculous. Thank you, God, I silently prayed.

The next morning I woke before the others. I went to the kitchen to make my coffee. It was something I did every morning of my life, but for some reason on this first day of the new millennium it was as if I was making coffee for the first time. Life and everything in it felt brand new. Like a new pair of shoes, it was not broken in yet, still squeaky and a little confining, yet willing to be formed to fit perfectly. I stood in the middle of this warm and cozy kitchen, the kitchen of a woman I'd never met, and cried. Thank you, thank you, thank you became my mantra that morning.

Miller spent three days in ICU, and then went back up to the Transplant Special Care Unit. There he would stay for two weeks. A few days after he was settled in his room I went home. I got home long enough to eat, sleep and wake up when the phone rang. It was the Coordinator on the transplant team. She told me Miller's new heart was leaking blood inside his chest and they were going back in that day. An hour later, I was in my car heading back to Cleveland.

With his typical sense of humor, Miller told me that before they wheeled him into the operating room he asked the doctors, "Okay, so which one of you did it?"

"Did what?" they asked.

"Lost his Rolex inside my chest?"

I got there before Miller came out of surgery. His recovery was harder this time than with the transplant and I watched helplessly as he twisted and turned in pain. I stayed with Jeff and Laura, but by the end of the week I became sick with the worst case of flu I'd ever had. I called Miller and told him I was going home.

For almost two weeks I battled the flu. I couldn't get out of bed. I had a sore throat, a terrible cough, no energy and no appetite. Miller on the other hand was doing great in Cleveland. The doctors couldn't believe his progress. Less than two weeks after I'd left, he was in the "P" Building as an outpatient. A week later, still weak and coughing, I drove back to pick him up.

The drive home was emotional for both of us. It was the first time he'd made the trip by car; for me I'd lost count and I-77 was as familiar to me as my own children's faces. The tears welled up in his eyes as we passed into North Carolina and we were both crying as we turned into our gravel driveway. Neither one of us could believe he was home.

In those first days home, to say we were happy would be an unfair understatement. Blissful comes closer to how we felt. We couldn't be away from each other.

We went everywhere together. We walked around the property. We sat in front of the fire. We talked and laughed and vowed we would never take each other or life for granted. We recounted our experience over and over as if to talk about it would somehow make it seem less like someone else's life and more like ours.

It was scary at first, being without doctors and nurses and the crash cart. But, by now we were old hands at medications and IVs, taking Miller's blood pressure and temperature. We kept a careful log of his vital signs and he made sure he took his medicine the same time each day. It didn't take long for us to get into a routine.

So now here I am almost one year to the day of Miller's death sentence. It's been the most remarkable year of my life. I sit at my same desk, looking at the same view, yet I am not the same person I was a year ago. I have changed in profound ways and in so many ways feel blessed by the experience. What have I learned? How am I different?

First and foremost I am truly aware that life is precarious at best. One day you're sitting in a golf cart, the next you're sitting in the ICU. Tragedy, hurt and pain don't just happen to someone else. They happen to us all. No one escapes. So do I wake up every morning expecting the other shoe to drop? Absolutely not! Now I appreciate each day more.

Miller and I sit in our two big Adirondack chairs, under a large beech tree, facing the mountains, and promise each other we will never not appreciate each day and what we have. We never want to forget what we've been through and what a gift each day really is. For that matter, what a gift each second, minute and hour really is.

Years ago I interviewed a cancer patient for a hospital brochure I was working on. She told me that since her diagnosis she saw life as if she were seeing it through a magnifying glass. She said everything about her life was larger and more finely detailed now. And even the smallest details caught her attention. I thought then I understood what she was talking about, but now I know I didn't fully get it. Now I do. When you are forced to face tragedy or crisis, you pay attention more, you're more aware of the fine points. After a while you don't just focus on the bad details but you start noticing the good and nurturing ones as well. The gentle trill of a warbler outside your window, the way cicadas start rattling faintly and build to a crescendo and then fade away again, the way the sun glows golden on green grass on a summer afternoon, the frail wet scent of honeysuckle in the morning, and how each morning you inhale the smell of coffee a little at a time until your whole body and mind are filled with it: this new-found awareness, I hope it never leaves.

Fear, doubt, and loss are still around. It's just how I deal with them that's changed. By facing the things I fear, I take away their power. By at least trying the things I think I cannot do, I give myself power. Doubt is diffused by faith, faith in myself and faith in a God who loves me. And by fully grieving for my losses and vowing to move forward instead of dwelling on them, I honor myself and lessen the pain of necessary leavings.

I don't fear death as much any more. As a hospice volunteer, I have been with patients in their lives and at their deaths. One thing I have learned from them is that they are not present at death. Their essence is gone, as if someone has invited them outside and they've gone and you can hear the screen door slam behind them. All that is left is their clothes and shoes and stuff. It's like when a hermit crab abandons its shell for a newer, larger one. When death came for them, it was a holy experience. It felt right.

But when death comes to your home like an uninvited guest who uses your stuff and sits in your favorite chair, it's a different story. That's how death came into our life. No matter how nice you are or how mean you become the fear of death will not leave, until you begin to respect its presence and willingly listen to those whose job it is to try to stop it before it goes any further. Only when you look death in the face and challenge it with all the strength you can muster, can you begin to cope with its presence in your life.

I'm more forgiving of others and myself now. Holding grudges just prevents me from fully experiencing the greatness of life. I don't wait or hesitate to tell and show the people I love, how much I love them. The people that don't enhance my life in a positive way, I sweep out of my mind with a broom of self-love. Life is too short not to surround yourself with the people you love and who love you back.

My priorities have shifted. Yes, my children and Miller are still a main concern of mine. But my creativity and need to creatively express myself have taken a giant step forward. I draw and paint more. I decoupage and do hand lettering. And I write for myself. I still sit on my patio and in front of my fireplace of a morning, I still garden and mix bath and beauty concoctions, I still meditate and pray and take naps, and I still cook and walk. All these things are ingrained in me now.

And I look at Miller, mowing the grass, eating dinner, flying a kite, or just walking across the pawnshop and I marvel at the miracle of organ transplantation. He is still my greatest inspiration and his donor is my greatest hero. What would it be like after Miller got his transplant? I used to think about this so many times on my way to Cleveland. Would I be home when I got the call? What would he be able to do? When would he come home and what was I supposed to do to get the house ready? I'd talked a little bit about this with the social worker but still felt uncertain.

So what's it really like? It's like having the old Miller back, only better. He wakes up happy and is as upbeat as ever. Yes, there's a lot of medicine, about 22 pills a day. But that's down from the 45 he took in the hospital. We laugh more and worry less. And I believe we both have a deeper relationship with God.

In an attempt to help others know the miracle of organ donation, we both became volunteers with Carolina Donor Services, our local procurement agency. We also wrote our donor's family a letter but unfortunately received word from LifeBanc of Ohio, the procurement agency serving Cleveland that the family wouldn't accept our letter. Actually, according to the procurement agency, only about 20 percent of recipients will ever meet or have contact with their donors' loved ones. We respect our donor's family's need for privacy and their need for time to fully grieve their loss.

I now have a greater empathy for the family members of the terminally ill or for anyone who's trying to make it alone. No one should suffer alone and as long as I have God I know I never will.

God's given me a great gift—the ability to see what my life would be like without the person I love the most and all the accoutrements that make my life mine. The gift is a deeper appreciation for them all. We set about creating a life for ourselves that eventually defines who we are and then we take for granted how extraordinary our life is. Sometimes we need a wake-up call.

Life is about opposites working together to make you whole. You can't see the light if you've never seen the dark. You can't be good if you don't know what bad is. And you can't fully experience the highest joys without fully delving into the deepest sorrows.

The first trip I made from Lenoir to Cleveland, Molly went with me. To get there from our house, you have to go through two tunnels, across two bridges and through three tollbooths. As we got inside the last tunnel and I saw the pinpoint of light ahead, I said to her, "Look Molly! There it is."

"What?" she asked.

"It's the light at the end of the tunnel," I replied laughing. She just rolled her teenage eyes at me. But, I felt the first glimmer of hope.

Throughout this experience I always felt like I was trying to get back to my life. That is, life the way it was before Miller got sick. It is only on looking back at my journey that I can see now that I was never going to go back to that other life. The whole time I was really moving forward toward a better one.

Afterword:
A Message from Miller

The first thing I remember thinking after I woke up from my transplant surgery was that I felt like a truck had hit me. The next thing was that for the first time in almost a year, I could hear the sound of my heart beating in my ears. I cried like a baby when I heard it.

Now, almost three years later, I can say in all sincerity, that my life is better than it ever was before the transplant. Tomorrow I visit Duke University Hospital, where I will have my biannual biopsy and other tests. Microscopic pieces of my heart will be removed and examined for any signs that my body may be rejecting it. In addition, I will have chest x-rays, an echocardiogram, and blood tests. Although I will always be grateful to the staff of the Cleveland Clinic, I am happy to be able to go to a hospital so close to home (about a three hour drive). I'm sure that my visit tomorrow will have the same positive results as those of the past. The doctors are still impressed by the strength of my new heart and my continuing good health. I still find it hard to believe I am living with someone else's heart.

A day does not go by that I don't think about and thank my donor and my donor's family. I will probably never get to thank them in person, but I pray for them to receive all the blessings God has to give, both on earth and in heaven.

I still think about and mourn the loss of the friends I made at The Cleveland Clinic, who didn't make it and for those friends from The Clinic that got hearts but didn't survive later on. I keep in touch with a few of the guys, mostly through Christmas cards, but they are on my mind often.

Lisa and I bought some beautiful, wooded property, high on a ridge, overlooking the valley and built a cozy home, where we live with our five dogs, two cats, a pair of geese and a duck. Marson and Molly work with me in the pawnshop and live nearby. When I'm not at work, I spend my time fishing in my little pond, taking care of the long gravel road to the house, or playing my guitar on the front porch, happy to be alive.

First, I would like to thank God for this second chance and for the knowledge he has bestowed on the men and women who make organ transplant possible.

What used to be an experimental procedure is now a viable treatment option and can save lives; more lives if only there were enough donors.

Second, I would like to thank my donor's family for having the love and courage to offer another person a second chance at life while under intense grief over their tremendous loss. Through me, they can know that their loved one lives on.

Third, I would like to thank my hero, my donor. I have never met you but through your heart I know something about you. You must have worked out regularly or been very health conscious, because from day one the surgeon and cardiologists of The Cleveland Clinic were impressed with the strength of your heart. I promise to continue to take good care of it.

Last, I must put it on record how grateful I am to my family and friends for their love and support before, during, and after the transplant. Friends like Jeff and Laura, who took such good care of Lisa, and the Wall family, who "adopted" Molly when she felt like her family was falling apart. I thank my brothers and sisters, brothers-in-law and sisters-in-law, cousins, aunts and uncles, and Lisa's mother and father, stand-ins for my deceased parents. And especially, thank you Lisa, Marson, and Molly. Without you, I could not have maintained any kind of positive attitude. You helped me hang on, especially when I thought my time was up. I'm not sure why I deserve this chance, but my promise to you is that I will make the most of it.

Tragically this summer, our friend Jay (Jeff's brother) lost his seventeen-year old son, Cliff. Cliff fell out of the back of a pick-up truck, leaving him "brain dead." I visited Jay and his family shortly after coming home from Cleveland. I went by to thank him for his help hooking Lisa up with Jeff and Laura in Hudson and sat in his living room talking to him, Genie (his wife), Cliff and Lauren (his daughter). Never in my wildest dreams would I have thought that this visit would come back to me in such a profound way.

When we found out about Cliff's accident we called Jay and learned that Cliff was an organ donor. "Your visit made such an impact on him, that he told me he decided to be an organ donor after you left us that night," recalled Jay. When we went to Cliff's funeral a few days later, we learned that because of this boy's courageous decision to be an organ donor four lives had been saved. I don't know if Jay will ever get to meet the recipient's of his son's precious organs or not, but I said thank you to him on their behalf.

Before my transplant I took so much for granted. Now, I try to appreciate every minute. I don't think about if I'll ever need another transplant or if my body decides one day to reject my new heart. I just live one day at a time, grateful that the generosity of others and the marvels of medical technology have allowed me to experience a miracle.

Miller H. Nance
September 15, 2003

Bibliography

Barber, Karen B. *Ready, Set, Wait...Help For Life On Hold.* Michigan: Baker Books, 1996.

Dickinson, Emily. *Selected Poems.* New York: Random House, 1993.

Kübler-Ross, Elisabeth. *On Death and Dying.* New York: Simon & Schuster, 1969.

Millay, Edna St. Vincent. *Collected Poems.* New York: Harper & Row, 1945.

SARK. *Transformation Soup.* New York: Simon & Schuster, 2000.

0-595-29772-2